MW01195293

STONE HOUSES
A DESIGN &
CONSTRUCTION HANDBOOK

STONE HOUSES
A DESIGN &
CONSTRUCTION HANDBOOK

BY STEVE PARSONS

TAB TAB BOOKS Inc.

BLUE RIDGE SUMMIT, PA. 17214

FIRST EDITION

SECOND PRINTING

Copyright © 1984 by TAB BOOKS Inc.
Printed in the United States of America

Reproduction or publication of the content in any manner, without express
permission of the publisher, is prohibited. No liability is assumed with respect to
the use of the information herein.

Library of Congress Cataloging in Publication Data

Parsons, Steve.
Stone houses.

Includes index.
1. Stone houses—Design and construction.   I. Title.
TH4818.S75P37   1984   690'.837   84-8729
ISBN 0-8306-0551-7
ISBN 0-8306-1551-2 (pbk.)

Contents

Introduction

THIS BOOK IS WRITTEN FOR THOSE WHO WISH TO build their own house, or for those who are contemplating the idea of building. We believe that anyone who wants their own home can, with determination, build a quality house that satisfies their needs, despite limited funds.

We built our house, doing everything ourselves, for $7,000. That included the interior finishing, wiring, plumbing (including pump, tank, and all piping), and a new stove. This amount is perhaps less than a down payment for a house that would meet your basic requirements. Money will be the prime determinant that will make or break your plans. Many of us have enough difficulty just earning sufficient income to meet our living expenses, without thinking of borrowing large sums of money to finance a new house.

Following the usual approach, you must have an approved building site and then, if you don't have a bulging bank account, you will have to set up a meeting with your local bank manager to discuss a loan. At this meeting, the manager or loans officer will want to know the nature of your project, its estimated cost, how it will be implemented, and how you will repay the loan.

If you want to build your house with your own hands, you might have difficulty explaining just how you cannot work (building your own house isn't gainful employment in the eyes of financial institutions) and yet repay your loan.

There is also the question of credibility as far as your skills as a builder are concerned. The bank will not want to hear that you are tackling a project as detailed as house building with minimal experience and only friends as co-workers. The possibilities of the bank cheerfully extending you a loan in these circumstances are scant. On the other hand, if you tell the bank that you are gainfully employed and plan to be into the distant future, that you are hiring qualified tradesmen to build your house, and that you will need three to four times the amount of money, your chances of getting a loan are much better.

Prior to building a house, we decided upon our priorities and goals and the best ways to attain them. We lived on a small farm mortgaged for

$16,000. We came to the farm from the city because we sought a life in the country, with fresh air, a garden, outdoor work, and a chance to test latent skills. We raised cattle and sold beef and cream. As the years passed, two things became apparent: we liked rural life very much and a lack of money was becoming a problem.

Two solutions faced us; either we could look for other jobs and try to accelerate mortgage and debt payments or we could sell. Full-time jobs meant a return to the city which, for us, was not really a choice at all. To sell meant we would be leaving our farm to pay off debts that, after seven years, had risen to $20,000 due to other commitments.

We sold, paid out $20,000 and were left with $7,000 and a piece of land from the farm acreage. Now we had to achieve a sense of independence and security as far as that is possible in our society. It meant building and owning our house completely, a large organic garden, a root cellar, the freedom to choose how to use our time to provide sustaining income.

To date we have accomplished these basic aims.

To build our house, including the interior finishing, cost $7,000.
The breakdown of costs was as follows:

80 bags cement @ $5 each:	$	400.00
4 loads each of sand & gravel:		200.00
Bulldozer:		300.00
Sawn lumber & logs:		1,000.00
Tools:		300.00
Gravel for road:		300.00
Nails:		150.00
Temporary power:		40.00
Electrical permit:		30.00
Electrical supplies:		500.00
Plumbing (Complete):		800.00
New Stove:		300.00
Stovepipe:		50.00
Roofing:		450.00
Wire:		30.00
Rebar:		50.00
Living and miscellaneous expenses:		1,400.00

Unexpected Expenses, Truck Engine:	500.00
Tax Bill	200.00
	$7,000.00

Two unexpected bills were for replacing an engine in our truck and a tax under a new local bylaw termed a "change of use" bill. When land changes from one classification to another, a tax is levied at 20 percent of assessed value. Land is classified as pasture, woodland, residential, cultivated, etc. Clearing our land changed it from woodlot to residential. Hence, a surprise bill for $200. When dealing with land taxes, be sure of all thorny areas.

Quality, we believe, means using the best materials (not the most expensive) solidly constructed with an outlook toward durability. Low maintenance should be a major design factor: re-roofing, painting, and replacing materials with short lifespans are expensive undertakings.

A functional house should be warm, free from draft and dampness, well lit with natural light, and designed to provide for not only the immediate but the ever changing needs of the builders. Incorporated into these basic criteria were various means of saving and distributing energy, plus any special provisions of the builders (workshop, sauna, music room, etc.).

With these ideas in mind, we examined various building materials. considering price, availability, quality, and maintenance factor. Materials commonly used include wood, brick, concrete, a variety of pressed woods (plywood, and chipboard, etc.), man-made plastic and aluminum sidings, asphalt shingles and galvanized steel roofing. All are costly and vary widely in quality and durability.

After due consideration of these factors, plus those of our building site, we arrived at the one material not listed—stone. It's true that in many parts of the world stone is a prime building material, but except for a few areas, it is not commonly used where we live despite being plentiful. We used only fieldstone, the ordinary stone found in roadside ditches, fields, and rockpiles. We used no quarried stone, and we did not split or shape a stone in any way.

Stone walls are strong, maintenance free,

basically unaffected by weathering, fireproof, and beautiful. Also, stone walls are not costly to build.

The biggest obstacle to overcome is the notion that building with stone is very hard work. Despite evidence to the contrary, many of our neighbors still hold this opinion. Wall construction work was done by my wife and myself, equally.

To build a stone house, or any house, requires time and patience, plus considerable planning. The actual length of time it takes to build a stone house depends upon its size, the number of builders, and, inevitably the weather. With the help of my brother, my wife and I built the walls of our house in two months, despite a summer of considerable rainfall. Our design allowed building to be spread over three years; thus, we built in one summer a house we could live in while we completed our plans for other sections. By doing this, we avoided the strain and pressures of attempting to build everything in one short summer, with the attendant possibility of failing in our plans to have a house to live in come winter.

We spent one enjoyable winter planning our house and making numerous drawings. As it turned out, this was time well spent. We began in April by clearing our lot and having the ground leveled. By October, the foundation and walls were complete and the roof went on very quickly.

This book can at least give you one method to fulfill your aspirations for a home, along with providing the satisfaction that comes with doing it yourself and exploring potentials. Good luck!

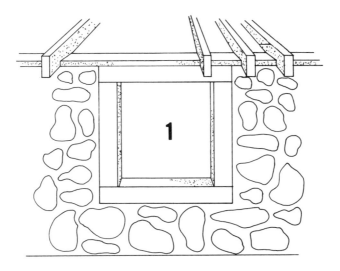

Preliminaries

THERE ARE SEVERAL WAYS TO GO ABOUT LOCATing your building site. The obvious initial method is to check the newspapers in the area in which you prefer to live. If you have a certain town or rural area in mind, send for the local newspaper there and consult the real estate ads, listed privately and by agencies.

The second method is the real estate agencies themselves. If you visit an agency, they will show you what they have listed for sale. Many agencies have a multiple-listing service. This means that the agency in your area will have listings of properties for sale in many other areas of the country besides their own territory. If you are interested in a site, go and inspect it. Remember that there may be a substantial mark-up in price to cover the agent's fee when dealing with an agency, but the agent often has a limit previously agreed upon with the owner, to which he can lower the price. So haggle a bit and get the best deal he can offer you.

A third method to purchase property is to watch the newspapers for listings of "Sheriff Sales."

These are sales of property by local governments which occur because the owners have failed to pay their taxes. Generally, these properties are auctioned off to the highest bidder, with the amount of taxes owed as the starting bid. Phone or write the sheriff's office for details of time and place for these auctions. You can inspect the property in advance of the sale and decide what it is worth to you. The drawback here is that land speculators will attend these auctions and often bid on a particularly good piece of property with the intention of keeping it for resale later when the value increases. But it's worth a try in any case.

The last method is by direct search. Get in your car, drive to the area you have chosen, and ask questions of the local residents. This is the method we used and it is how we originally found our property. If you see a piece of land with old tumble-down buildings, find out who owns it. Perhaps you can buy it, remove the buildings, and have an excellent ready-made site. The residents of any area often know of unlisted land for sale. They also are sometimes aware of those who are "thinking of selling" a piece of their large acreage and who will do so if you approach them courteously.

Before signing anything or writing out your check, however, you must have your mind reasonably settled on the following criteria.

● Is the site large enough to accommodate plans for expansion, such as a barn or garage?

● Can you have a garden?

● Are phone and electrical services available?

● Are roads accessible year round?

● What are the seasonal angles of the sun and how would your house be oriented to make the best use of the winter rays?

● What are the exposures to wind?

● Are there any negative features nearby; i.e., dumps, future subdivisions, etc.?

● What about sewage lines?

Most of these questions are easily answerable either on the site or by asking the local residents. Two factors of utmost importance are a plentiful source of good water and the type of soil.

WATER

A good water supply is crucial to your building plans and also to your future needs. If you are building in a rural area, can water be obtained from a dug well or a spring, or will you have to have a well drilled (which can be very costly)? Again, see how the local people get their water. If the majority of the residents have dug wells that provide ample, clean water, without going dry during a hot summer, then the chances of your site producing a similar well are good. A spring is also a good source of water, but have any water source tested by the department of health for purity. This is often done free. Also, check local ordinances concerning sources of water. You may have to tap into a municipal system regardless of the presence of water on your land.

A drilled well may be necessary if a dug well doesn't work. To do this, hire a contractor with a large machine to drill a hole deep into the earth and tap the water that lies below. Well drillers charge per foot of hole drilled and prices vary. Our well was drilled at $10 per foot to a depth of 65 feet, thus, a total cost of $650. I know of wells drilled to a depth of 250 feet, and 500 feet is not uncommon. There is

also usually no guarantee of water and some unfortunates have paid lavishly for a dry hole (Fig. 1-1).

To locate a source of water on your property, there are three things you can do. First, ask the former owner if he knows the location of any springs or other sources of water on the site; second, walk around and look; third, hire a dowser or do the dowsing yourself.

Chances are the former owner will know of any springs or wet spots. To have a spring on your land is a bonus. Springs are initially formed when melting snow and rain water sink through the ground and porous layers of rock until they are stopped by an impenetrable layer. The water collects and forms an underground storage basin that follows the layer of rock until it emerges, sometimes many miles from its source. It comes bubbling up from the ground, often from a rock outcropping, clear and cold. A good spring will keep issuing water during a dry spell when ordinary dug wells have long dried up. Our forefathers usually knew the location of all the springs in their area, how fast they flowed, and if they had ever gone dry.

A wet spot on your land can indicate an area where water collects naturally or it could also indicate a spring under the ground. You have to dig to find out. A dug well is made by digging a hole in the ground, either by hand or machine, until ample water begins to fill it up. Dug wells can be as shallow as 6 feet or go down for 50 feet or more. In arid parts of the world, a 150 foot well is commonplace. Next, the hole is lined with stone or concrete tile, the bottom is graveled, and a cover is built. A spring-fed well does not go dry as quickly as a well fed by groundwater.

The purification of well water occurs when it filters through the soil and layers of rock. Spring water and water from a drilled well are very often of good quality because of the depth from which they issue, but water from a dug well must be carefully monitored, especially during the warm season, because it can "go bad" as our neighbors put it. This means high levels of bacteria build up in the water because of the heat and no input of fresh water from rain or snow. In these instances, drinking water must be obtained elsewhere. Sadly, even the deep

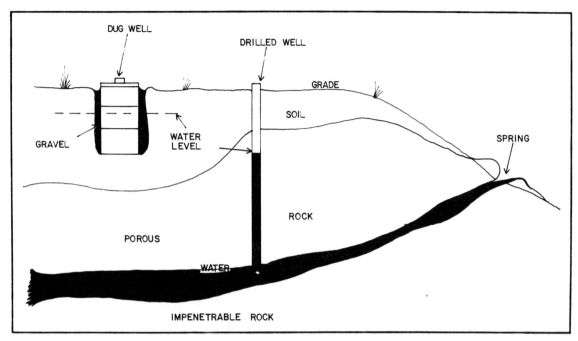

Fig. 1-1. Common rural water sources include dug wells, drilled wells, and springs. Drilled wells and springs emanate from deep subterranean water. A dug well is fed by the water table, or surface water. Purification is accomplished by filtration of water through the soil. A dug well fed by a spring is less likely to go dry than one fed by surface water.

subterranean sources of water are becoming polluted due to modern toxic chemicals that find their way through the earth. It is our hope that this process will not reach the horrific proportions envisioned by many environmentalists.

Dowsing is a well established method of locating water. It has a long history and its origin is open to discussion. The main points are these. The dowser uses a forked stick, shaped somewhat like an oversize slingshot, to do his work. He grasps it with both hands, the tail of the slingshot away from his body, and walks methodically over your land. Suddenly, the tip of the stick will bend towards the earth, sometimes with great force. There is water where it points.

From the force of the bending, a good dowser can tell how much water there is and how deep to dig to reach it. Magic? It seems so at first sight and there are many, very vocal skeptics, but it's worth looking into. Like acupuncture, dowsing is becoming accepted as fact, and there are schools to teach both throughout North America. A good dowser

will tell you it takes experience to accurately locate water and estimate its amount. I have been told that most people are capable of dowsing, but some are better than others. Ask the neighbors for the name of a good dowser. You'll probably be surprised at how easy it is to locate one.

SOIL

The type of soil must also be determined. To build a stone house, or any house, over swampy land is to invite disaster. Some soils, such as shale or hard clay, are very well suited to building because they will support a great deal of weight without settling. Other soils, such as wet sand or soft clay, are less so.

The drainage factor is related to soil type. Clay soils do not readily absorb water whereas sandy soils do; hence clays stay drier.

It's a simple matter to determine the type of soil on your site. Just dig several widely spaced holes and examine the results. Soil composition varies widely in many areas, and where we live our

3

soil is hard clay. By going less than one-quarter mile from our site, the soil becomes hard shale and in another direction it becomes soft clay.

Examine your land carefully to determine its soil type. The very best foundation for a stone house is bedrock or *ledge* as it's sometimes termed. The next in line are shale and gravel soils; then on down through hard, dry clay and sand; and finally, soft sand and clays. Soil type determines the size of the *footing* (concrete support) you will require for your house. The harder the soil the smaller the footing and vice versa. If in doubt concerning the soil composition, you can have it analyzed by any local agricultural agency or you could ask a local farmer or building contractor. You'll be sure to receive plenty of advice.

Examine the details of your proposed site, looking for such things as rock protruding through the ground surface (indicating bedrock). Drive an iron bar into the ground in several places to get an idea of soil depth and compactness. If you eventually want a garden, look for a suitable location and use the iron bar to probe for large boulders.

Soil type plus the contours of the land are to be considered when predetermining the location of your septic field. (Presuming of course there is no public sewage hookup.) The septic system will be receiving the waste water from your sinks, as well as the toilet system, and it must distribute it away from your source of drinking water. It must also not be allowed to flow toward any neighbor's well or spring.

Thus the topography of your site must be examined. Where are the high and low spots? Is your site flat or does it have an overall slope? If so in which direction? By walking around your site, you can mentally place the location of your house, well, and septic system. How about the orientation to the sun after these aspects have been settled? Can you manage some south-facing windows?

The lay of the land must be studied so you will also know the direction of water runoff during the spring thaw and seasonal rainstorms. Obviously, it should be away from your house. That sleepy hollow so picturesque in midsummer may be a shallow pond in early spring.

It's a good idea to examine your lot during a heavy rain. We did just that one day in early spring. Donning raincoats and boots we walked around our site between the closely spaced trees and tried to extend our imaginations to the day when the lot would be cleared, the house facing south with the garden to the west. We saw a spot where it appeared to be swampy and holding water so we changed our location for the house. We spent several hours in the heavy rain with water dripping down our necks, holding lively discussions on the garden spot, the location of the driveway, and how to avoid cutting one stately oak tree.

From that examination came the final decisions that situated our house on the lot. The small, swampy area now borders our driveway. We let the water stay and in turn we are seranaded each spring by a multitude of chirping frogs. Growing in the wet area are blue irises, lily-of-the-valley, and other moisture-loving plants.

LEGALITIES

Legal matters are essential considerations. Is it permissible to build on your site? Will the local authorities grant you a building permit? Will the department of health grant permission to install a septic system? If so what are their requirements? The answer to this last question could end your plans immediately with prohibitive costs.

Building Codes

Often when inquiring into the legal aspects of building, it becomes necessary to submit your house plans to various departments for their scrutiny. Usually they are interested in the size of the house, its layout with regard to the site, distances between any well and septic systems, and other factors depending on the local bylaws (Fig. 1-2).

The days are fairly well past when any hopeful house builder could erect the castle of his or her dreams without considering the wishes of the local town or city council. Once the basic laws are

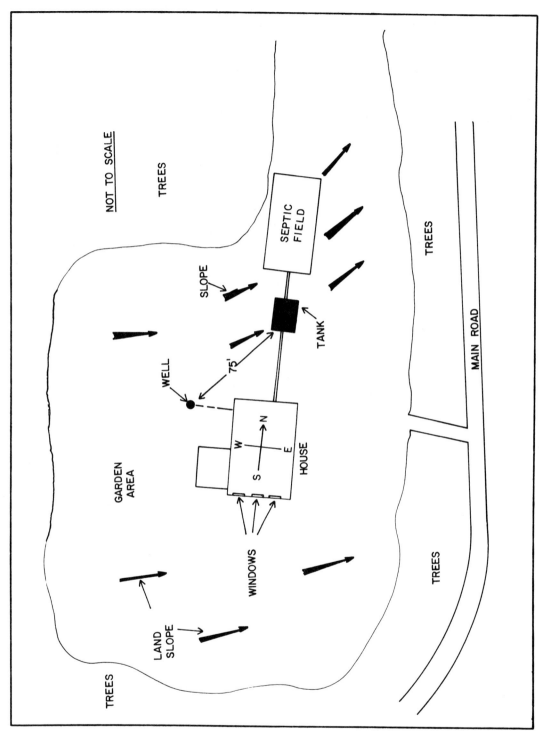

Fig. 1-2. A layout drawing for house and septic system in relation to land slope and compass points. Often required by government before various building permits are issued. Note that the direction of water flow is away from the well and at least 75 feet apart.

known, then you can consider ways to design your house that will conform to their requirements and still have the leeway to indulge your imagination. Nothing would be worse than to have half your walls erected only to be ordered to cease building immediately. It has happened.

Depending upon where you live, the building codes and bylaws will vary in their requirements. Get copies of the building codes and the legal prerequisites of the department of highways, the department of health, the electrical power company, and so on. It will sometimes seem as though the effort to discover and comply with the laws of the government is more difficult than the actual construction, but it is all necessary and has to be investigated before proceeding. Don't despair. If others can build their own houses, so can you.

Septic Systems

The department of health will be especially specific in their requirements for a septic system. First of all, they will usually want to conduct a *percolation test* on your site (Fig. 1-3). This tests the capability of your soil to absorb and disperse water. This capability is measurable and is called *rate of percolation*. Two or three holes, 1 foot in diameter, are dug in the area where you plan to locate your *dispersal field* (waste water disposal). They are dug to the depth of your planned installation and filled with about 1 foot of water. This sweeps away and is replaced with more water until a constant rate of seepage is established. Then the time in minutes is measured for the water level to drop 1 inch. This is checked several times. From this test, the department of health determines the size of the tank

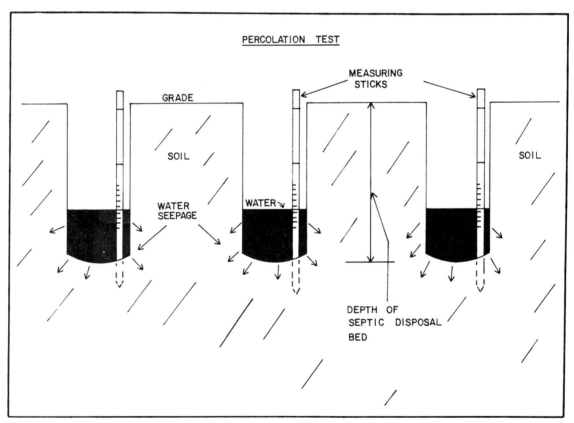

Fig. 1-3. A percolation test is usually required by the department of health for a permit authorizing the building of a septic field. Water is poured into several test holes dug at the site and, when a constant seepage is established, the dispersal time is measured by observing dropping water level on a measuring stick. This determines the size of septic tank and dispersal bed.

needed and its accompanying disposal bed. Clay soils have a slow percolation rate and sandy soils are faster. If your soil is suitable, then you are given a permit to proceed.

A snag arises if you want to build on a rocky site or where the soil depth is shallow. You will either be refused a permit or instructed to have earth hauled in to build a disposal field to a measured depth. It goes without saying that this can be expensive.

Depending upon where you live, however, you may be able to build a *composting toilet* that would be acceptable to the department of health and which eliminates the need for a large sewer system.

Composting toilets are sold commercially and work by mixing the waste with earth and other biodegradables such as hay or straw. A bacteria is added to hasten the decomposition of the mixture. This eventually results in a black, loamy material, devoid of noxious odors, that is a great fertilizing agent for plants. Information is readily available on these toilets, including instructions for building your own.

Deeds

If you have proceeded thus far with favorable results, the final consideration is that of *title* to your land. Your deed.

A clear title is a must. This means that no long-lost relative of the previous owner of your land is going to appear on your doorstep one day with a claim of ownership to your property. It can happen and it has happened. That is why land deals are done using the services of a lawyer. The lawyer checks the land title at the county recording office and guarantees that you know all the details of the transaction you are entering into. It is possible to check the title yourself for a small charge but, unless you are very careful and methodical, it is worth paying the lawyer's fee for the resulting peace of mind. Try to find a lawyer who is practiced in land transactions and thoroughly competent. Don't be afraid to ask questions and shop around. If a lawyer won't take the time to answer your questions now, chances are he won't be too thorough on

your behalf later.

DESIGN

If you have designed your house before going site hunting, you need only modify anything that needs to be changed to suit the location. House design and the features of the site obviously go hand in hand.

In our case, we had several ideas in hand regarding the design of our house that we expanded upon after we had chosen the site.

Let me emphasize one fact. You cannot spend too much time planning. The extra time spent upon your designs and layouts will greatly minimize later frustrations and costly mistakes. We spent one winter reading and digesting books on design until we had condensed all our concerns into a basic plan. Our decision was to build a small, complete house on which we would add, in subsequent summers, further additions. So we began drawing.

A good way to start is with a floor plan. First get used to drawing to scale. Buy some graph paper with ¼-inch squares and choose a scale (¼ inch to 1 foot is handy). This will give you a clear insight into the actual dimensions of your house. Draw your furniture to scale in the various rooms of the house. This will show you the space available between walls and beds, where the stove will fit, how much space for sinks is available, and so on. We suggest you read some books on basic house design from which you can glean the ideas most useful to you (Fig. 1-4).

Once the floor plan is generally established, draw the house from its various perspectives: front, rear, and sides, including doors, windows, and any other necessary features. The idea is to get a "feel" for the total structure in three dimensions. You could also build a small scale model using stiff cardboard. By doing this, you might discover one or more major obstacles not easily noticed from the floor plans (Figs. 1-5 through 1-9).

The designing of a house includes not only the floor plan but also the *substructure* or foundation, the walls, roof, interior finishing, wiring, and plumbing layouts. Beginning with the foundation, I'll explain how each aspect of the house was designed and then actually built.

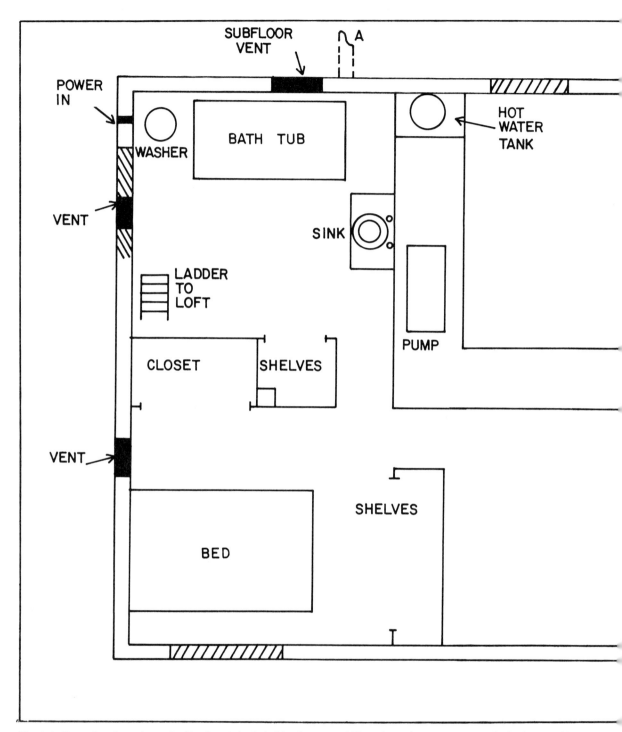

Fig. 1-4. Floor plan drawn to scale. Furniture is included to give a good idea of spacing arrangements in the house. Also incuded are sub-floor vents and entrance for electrical power.

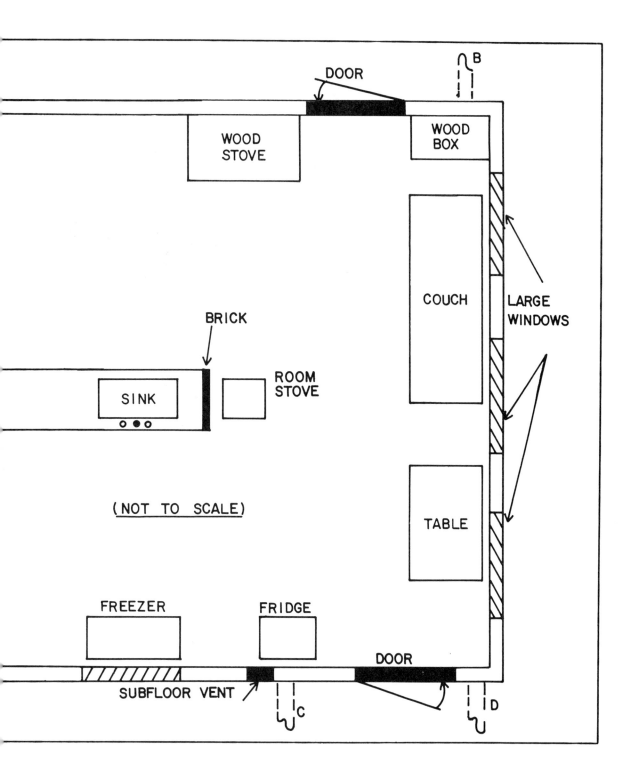

DOOR

B

WOOD
STOVE

WOOD
BOX

BRICK

LARGE
WINDOWS

SINK

ROOM
STOVE

COUCH

(NOT TO SCALE)

TABLE

FREEZER

FRIDGE

DOOR

SUBFLOOR VENT

C

D

9

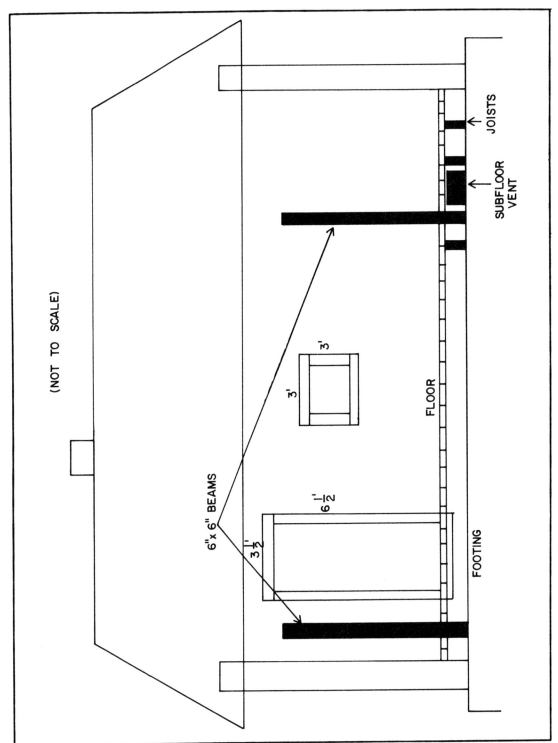

(NOT TO SCALE)

6" x 6" BEAMS

3'

3'

6 1/2'

3 1/2'

FLOOR

FOOTING

JOISTS

SUBFLOOR
VENT

Fig. 1-5. East view of our stone house. Note 6 × 6 beams installed as junction points for the walls of a planned addition.

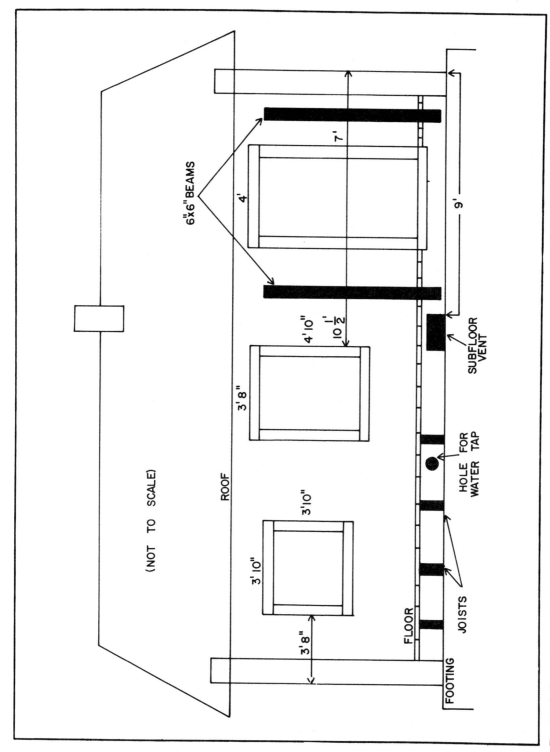

(NOT TO SCALE)

6"x6" BEAMS

ROOF

7'

9'

4'

4'10"

10 1/2"

3'8"

SUBFLOOR VENT

HOLE FOR WATER TAP

3'10"

3'10"

FLOOR

JOISTS

3'8"

FOOTING

Fig. 1-6. In the west view, all horizontal distances are carefully marked and wall openings for vents and outside tap are indicated. The 6 × 6 beams are for the addition of a porch.

11

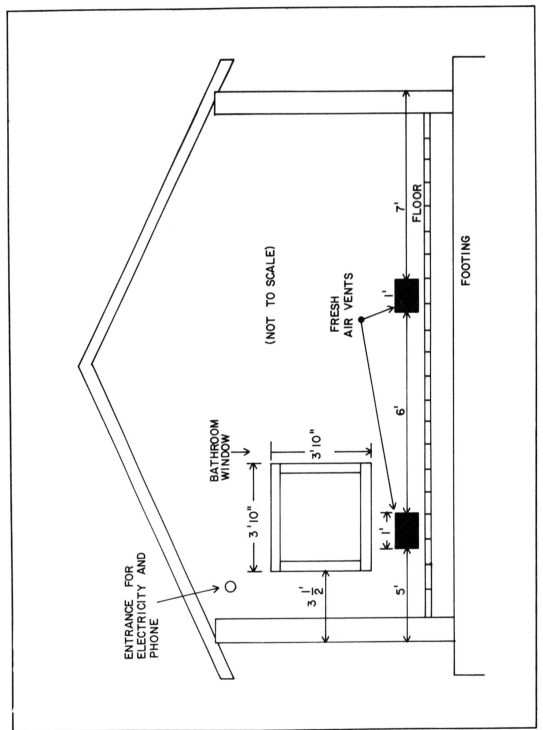

Fig. 1-7. North view showing the 1 × 1-foot vents in the stone walls. These adjustable vents open inside the house, just above floor level, to admit cool air. In winter they are sealed off.

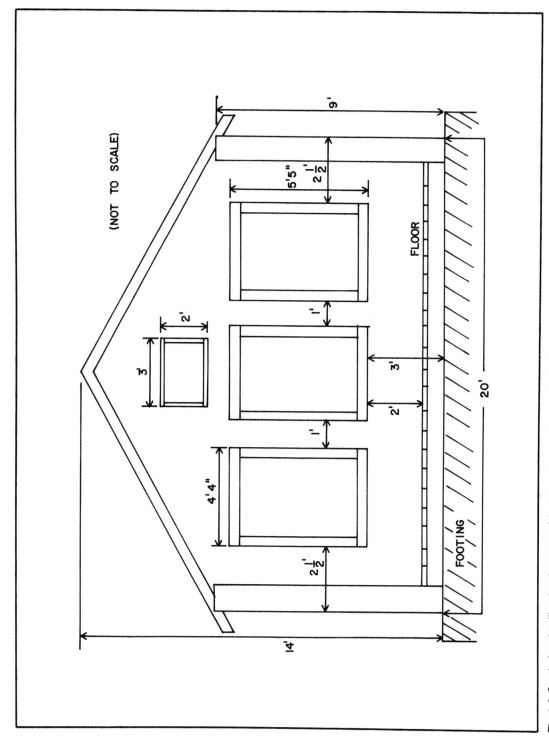

(NOT TO SCALE)

Fig. 1-8. South view detailing the placement of the large windows. The smaller 2 × 3-foot window in the peak serves as part of the air flow system; two smaller 1 × 1-foot vents initiate air flow from north wall. Warm air escapes via the south window, which opens outward and is hinged at the top.

13

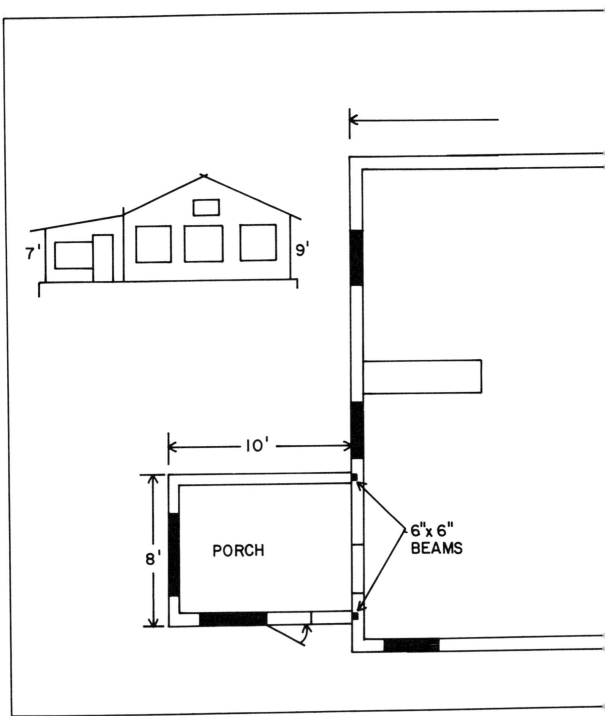

Fig. 1-9. Floor plan and front elevation drawing indicating layout. Included are the 8 × 10 porch on the west side and the third and final addition of a 12 × 18 section on the east.

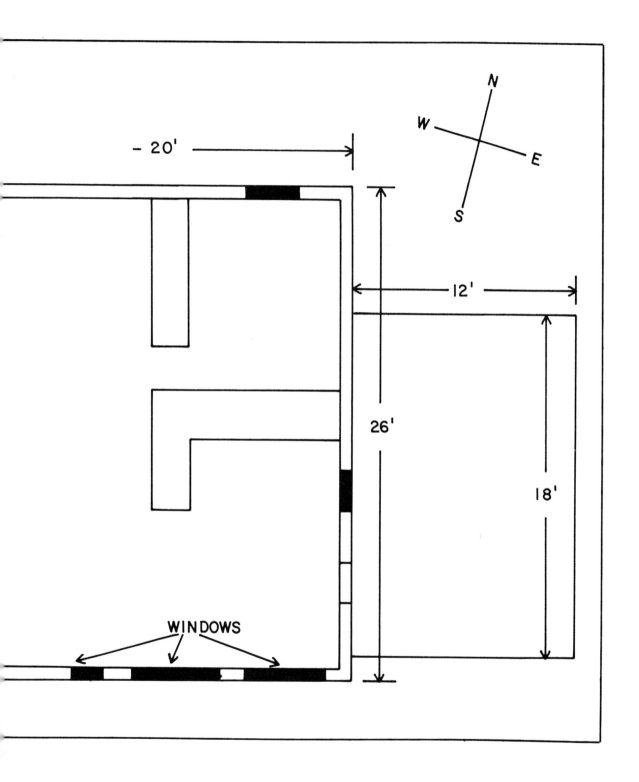

WINDOWS

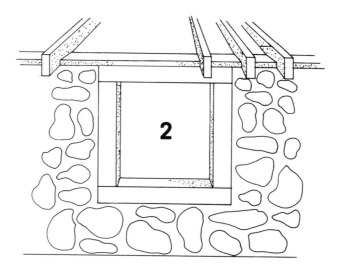

Foundation

THE FOUNDATION IS THE BACKBONE OF YOUR house. The house is supported by its foundation, and the stability of the house is directly proportional to the size and strength of its foundation. A weak foundation, or one that is heaved by frost, will crack, settle, and cause walls to buckle, floors to sag, and roofs to bow inwards.

Foundations are constructed using standard procedures. For example, a wood frame house with a basement follows this procedure: a large hole is dug, wooden forms are placed, and a low, solid concrete wall is poured. This is called the *footing* and varies in size depending upon house dimensions. Upon the footing, the basement walls are erected using either concrete blocks, or solid concrete (Fig. 2-1). The wood frame house is then built on these walls, which are called the foundation. Thus the total foundation, in this instance, includes the footing plus the concrete walls.

If there is no basement, the following method may be used. A footing is poured and the walls of the house, which in this case are made of stone and concrete, are built directly on top. The space be-

tween the floor and the ground is called a *crawl space* (Fig. 2-2).

Still another method eliminates the crawl space by pouring a solid concrete floor called a *slab* floor. A wood floor can be built on top of the slab if desired and insulation installed to make it warmer (Fig. 2-3).

Other types of foundations also exist, such as concrete posts or treated wooden posts, which are sunk into the ground. The house sits on large beams that rest upon the concrete posts. This obviously cannot be used for a stone house, or for a house in which you want a basement. Where this is used for a wood house, the footing and concrete foundation are eliminated (Fig. 2-4).

DESIGN

In order to design the foundation you must know the dimensions of the house, type of floor you will have, where the well and septic system will be, and whether or not you want a full basement, partial, or crawl space.

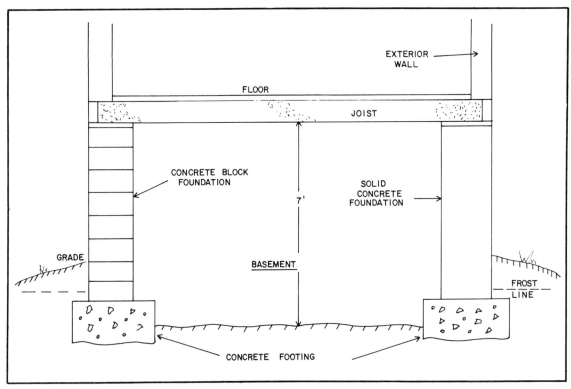

Fig. 2-1. Structure of a basement for a frame house. Concrete foundation walls may be made of mortared concrete blocks or solid concrete, sitting on a concrete footing extending below frost line. The floor and walls rest on top of walls.

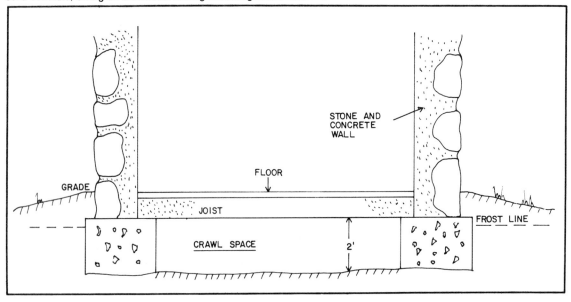

Fig. 2-2. A stone house without a basement. The walls sit directly on the footing to form a crawl space under the floor. The floor is a traditional wood floor of 2 × 8-inch joists and a subfloor of 1-inch lumber.

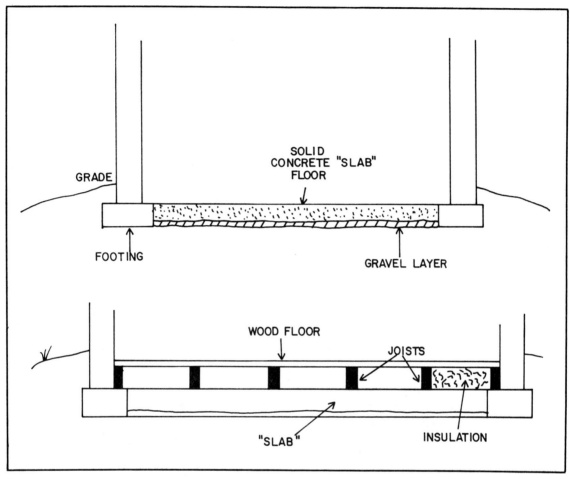

Fig. 2-3. Diagram of a slab floor with no basement or crawl space. Solid concrete is poured inside the footing. To cover the slab floor, wood joists can be laid and then covered. This floor may be insulated between the joists with fiberglass for additional warmth.

It's possible to have a full basement in a stone house but the design parameters are altered from that of a house with only a partial basement or crawl space. A full basement means extensive excavation, a much larger footing plus thicker walls to support the heavy stone work, more expense, and the terrain must be suitable for installing it (Fig. 2-5).

A full basement requires a very large hole to be dug and to do it by hand is a herculean task. It is a job for heavy equipment such as a back-hoe or bulldozer.

The walls of the house will be much higher with a full basement, in the range of 15 feet and therefore the footing must be much larger to adequately support them. The walls themselves must also be thicker due to the increased weight. Twelve-inch walls are a minimum and 14-inch walls are better. Also, making extra concrete plus hiring the bulldozer can be very expensive if you have limited funds.

The final and most important aspect to be considered is the terrain. If drainage is poor, then the basement will always collect water. Water in a

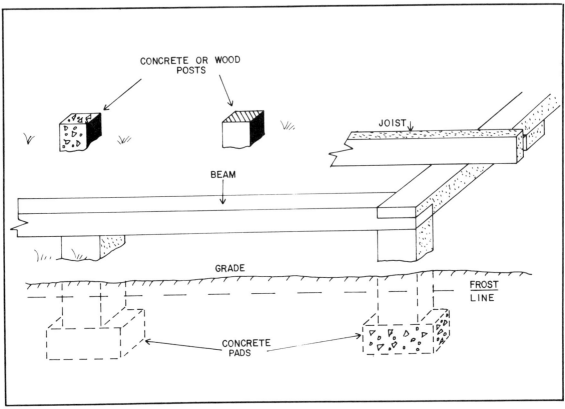

CONCRETE OR WOOD POSTS

JOIST

BEAM

GRADE

FROST LINE

CONCRETE PADS

Fig. 2-4. A post and beam foundation is made by laying large beams on concrete posts poured in holes in the ground. The posts can also be of wood, treated with a preservative. This method is suitable for houses that require no basement or crawl space, such as a cottage, but impossible for use with a stone house.

basement means dampness and mold, thus defeating the whole purpose of having a basement in the first place.

Before deciding to build a basement, consider carefully the reasons why you want it. We discussed the arguments, pro and con, for a basement and the cons won out. Reasons for having one were that it would provide space to store food, store firewood, have a workshop, install a furnace and pump, put a laundry room, and it would keep the floors warm in winter. Reasons against it were the magnitude of the labor to build it, the cost, and our terrain (projections of bedrock). Also we learned, from having a basement on our farm, that firewood cures 100 percent better where there is a circulation of air. Our furnace wood was kept in the base-

ment and the stove wood in the woodshed outdoors. The stove wood dried faster and burned better than the furnace wood. (Some wetter species of wood actually mildewed in the basement.)

As for food storage, a basement, unless it's unheated, is just too warm. Root crops such as carrots, turnips, and potatoes and other crops such as apples and cabbage will not keep nearly as long as they will in a separate, outdoor root cellar. Also, an unheated basement will not keep the floors warm. To be fair, you can build a separate root cellar in your basement, provided it is well insulated and vented to the outside air.

As a workshop location, I find a basement unsuitable because I like lots of natural light plus a view, neither of which the average basement can

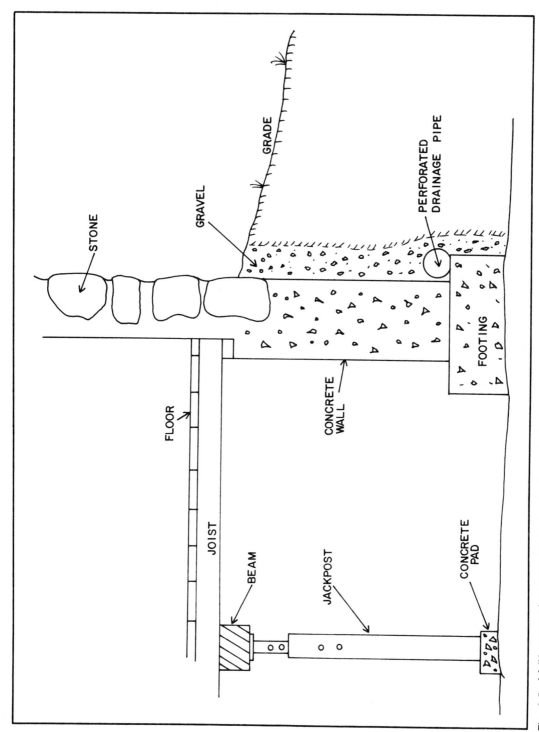

Fig. 2-5. A full basement for a stone house showing the method of backfilling the walls. A metal jackpost supports floor joists. The walls are thick where they begin at the footing and narrow where the floor rests and exterior walls begin. Width of above-ground walls is at least 10 inches.

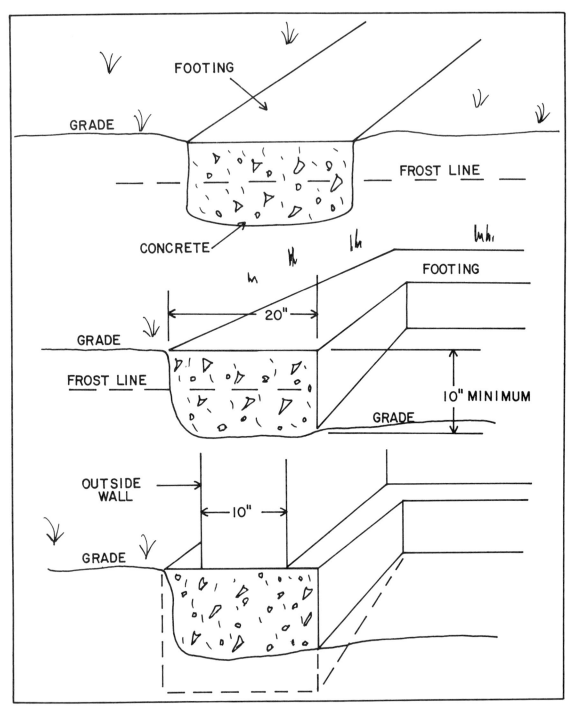

Fig. 2-6. A concrete footing poured below the frost line, the average depth of frost penetration during the winter. Footing should be, vertically, at least as thick as the width of the walls to be built on it; and horizontally, at least twice as wide as the walls to be built.

22

supply. Furnaces and pumps can be installed in crawl spaces, or even at floor level, and floors can be kept warm by means other than a full basement, as discussed in Chapter 6.

So for our design we chose a 2-foot crawl space with a standard wood floor using 2 × 8 foot joists. The crawl space enabled us to install the plumbing under the floor. It is out of the way and yet accessible if need be. With a slab floor, the plumbing is pre-built and covered with poured concrete or hidden in the woodwork of the house and under a wooden floor.

(It is quite possible to dig a hole of 8 × 10 feet under one part of the house for a storage cellar, but you must be absolutely certain you are not digging a pond. Drainage must be adequate to do this. We built a separate root cellar in the side of a small hill where the temperature is more suitable to storage of food than that of a warmer storage area under the house.)

When designing your footing there is a rule of thumb which states the footing should be, in vertical height, at least as high as the thickness of the walls built on it. Horizontally (width), it should be twice as thick as the walls. Thus, 10-inch walls require a minimum footing 10 inches thick and 20 inches wide (Fig. 2-6).

This rule is for standard, wood frame housing. A contemporary house generally has 6- to 7-foot high concrete basement walls and so, if your stone house has no basement, the rule will also apply because your walls will be similar in overall weight.

Fig. 2-7. The slipforms placed on finished footing. Note stones placed inside footing for use on walls.

(A wood frame house has basement walls, plus the wood framing and roof; whereas a stone house has only the walls and roof.)

The size of the footing also depends upon the load-bearing capability of the soil on your site. As previously mentioned, some soils will support much more weight than others. The load-bearing capacity of soils can be ascertained by asking a local contractor or land survey department.

Our solution to the problem was relatively simple since our land is a mixture of hard clay and bedrock. We built a footing 20 inches wide. The depth varied where we encountered bedrock, sometimes as little as 12 inches down (Fig. 2-7). We cleaned exposed bedrock of earth using a brush and water and poured the concrete for the footing

directly on the rock. Where we encountered hard clay, we dug to a depth of 3 feet or more. As a result, our footing is quite thick in some places. Our neighbor, the farmer, came to view our footing upon its completion. His comment was: "Now that's what I call an able footing."

If you are building where the ground is soft, a wider footing may be necessary. Remember that overbuilding is better than underbuilding, particularly in the supporting structure for your house.

The footing is a mixture of concrete and stone plus reinforcing bars. These steel rods are inserted in the footing while it's being made. Standard procedure is to use ½ to ⅝-inch rod laid lengthwise in the footing, about 2 inches from the bottom and spaced 6 to 8 inches apart (Fig. 2-8). These rods

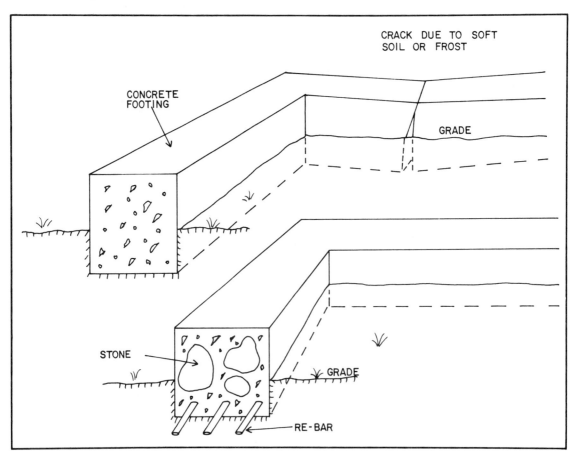

Fig. 2-8. Footings, if not built below the frost line, are susceptible to cracking from frost heave. If not properly reinforced they may settle or become cracked. Reinforcing bar is installed near the bottom of the footing to greatly strengthen concrete.

Fig. 2-9. Partially completed footing with forms still in place. Note pieces of steel and large stones to anchor future walls.

make the footing structurally stronger and prevent it from cracking vertically, thus cracking the walls and altering the rest of the house. Reinforcing rod is expensive but fortunately there are alternatives, limited only by your searching abilities. Railway track, truck axles, angle iron, pieces of old farm machinery and so on can be used, provided they are not hopelessly rusty (Fig. 2-9).

The footing must extend below the *frost line* in your area to prevent cracking of the footing due to frost heave. This occurs when water from melting snow or condensation collects under the footing and then freezes. The expanding ice crystals have tremendous power and can easily snap a footing in two, even with the house on top of it. The frost line is the average depth to which frost penetrates the earth in winter. To determine this figure for your area, consult the records kept by the nearest weather bureau. They will have all sorts of statistics that go back a century or more. You can also ask any farmer about frost and receive an answer that will probably be just as accurate. If you find the average frost penetration for your locale to be 2 feet, then go down 3 feet for safety.

TOOLS

To build a footing you will need tools and materials. Many of the tools required are basic to any type of construction and will serve you well for years. It's fun to collect them while you are still planning your house. You have ample time to spend looking for tools at garage sales, flea markets, and in the want ads. Don't buy broken or badly worn tools. Likewise, avoid tools that are not well made. They will break and cost you more in the long term. Take good care of your tools and don't leave them exposed to the elements. Oil any wooden handles with linseed oil to make the wood resist water. They will be easier on the hands because they won't swell, crack, and become rough (Table 2-1). Keep your edged tools sharp and they will make your work much easier.

Before we began construction, we had many tools that we gathered over the years. Yet it became necessary to buy some new ones to meet the demands of building. A 50-foot tape is necessary for

Table 2-1. List of Basic Tools.

PICK	WHEELBARROW
SHOVELS	CEMENT MIXER
TROWELS	LADDER
TAPE MEASURES	WIRE BRUSH
(50' AND 12')	SPONGE
LEVEL (3')	RUBBER GLOVES
CHALK LINE	BUCKETS
HAMMERS	(METAL)
WRECKING BAR	MALLEABLE WIRE
WIRE CUTTERS	REINFORCING BAR (1/2")
PLIERS	
CROSSCUT SAW	
1/4" DRILL	
HACKSAW	
SQUARE	
WRENCH	

MATERIALS FOR FOOTING

LUMBER	NAILS (DOUBLE-HEADED)
SAND	CLEAN STONES
GRAVEL	1/2" RE-BAR
CEMENT	
CLEAN WATER	

laying out the house dimensions and checking the forms for accuracy before pouring any concrete. We used it constantly.

A level is also a must. You will need it throughout the building process from footing to interior finishing. Don't skimp on a level. Get one at least 4 feet long for the large jobs such as leveling the footing and the walls. For smaller things like checking window frames, a 2½- or 3-foot level is fine.

A chalkline will be needed wherever a long straight line has to be marked, such as inside a form to indicate where the concrete will stop, or to mark a board lengthwise for cutting.

Wire cutters are required to cut the malleable wire used to fasten wood forms together. Get a pair of good quality steel, otherwise they become dull, wear gaps in their edges, and cause you to grit your teeth a lot when using them.

Saws, hammers, drills and a framing square

are necessary to do any type of woodworking. Try to obtain a crosscut saw (for cutting boards across the grain), a rip saw (for cutting lengthwise) and, if you can manage, a circular saw (the electric saws with the round blades). As for the other tools, buy quality items. They are worth it.

A wheelbarrow, even two, is needed constantly to ferry the large quantities of sand and gravel to the mixing area. Don't buy a garden variety wheelbarrow. They have little narrow hard rubber tires and trying to maneuver a heavy load of concrete or gravel over rough or muddy ground puts on quite a show for any bystanders. Chances of a successful trip without an upset are slim. Of course, you can always wheel it over a highway of boards laid end to end on the ground, as we did, but the chances improve only marginally. The large, heavy-duty wheelbarrows with fat inflated tires are best. We obtained one at long last and now wonder how we managed without it.

A cement mixer is an added bonus. It's possible to mix all the concrete by hand, in a wooden box called a *cement trough,* but a mixer is faster and definitely easier. Also, a mixer does a thorough job of blending all the ingredients in the mix, whereas by hand it becomes a laborious procedure. Shop around for a secondhand mixer, but remember you will need temporary electrical power hooked up before you can use an electric mixer.

Ladders become necessary as the stone walls go up. You will need them to erect staging and carry rocks and cement. The best type are stepladders since they are stable and self-supporting. An extension or painter's ladder is more difficult to use. For our project, however, we used both types, but the stepladder got 90 percent of the use.

A wire brush is used to clean any moss and dirt from stones. A sponge is used to wet the stones before putting them in concrete (wet stones make a better bond). Rubber gloves are used while working with the concrete by hand. (Concrete contains ingredients that are harmful to bare skin over a prolonged period of contact.)

Buckets are used to carry water and also wet concrete. Metal buckets are preferable because they will take much more abuse than plastic ones, which tend to bend under pressure. Their handles rip from the sockets at inopportune moments such as when you are teetering atop a ladder and trying to pass the bucket to your mate.

SITE PREPARATION

Finally the day came when we arrived at our site to begin work. (If your site is a semi-level field with a convenient slope you are lucky. If not, there will be some preliminary preparations to be made. There may be trees to be cut down and cleared away. If you do this yourself, stack the wood in piles after cutting it in 4-foot lengths and then gather and burn the remaining brush. You can use the wood yourself as firewood or sell it.) We cut four cords of wood while clearing our lot, more than half of our winter firewood needs. We didn't cut any more trees than were necessary to give space for our house and garden. Stumps then had to be removed and the earth leveled or *graded.*

Grading is best done by machine, and the cost is definitely worth it. If the stumps are large, they are virtually impossible to remove by hand. The bulldozer will remove the stumps and also the top level of soil where an interlacing network of roots makes digging very hard indeed.

Once this work was done it became necessary to make a driveway before we could proceed. The road into our site was little more than a passage cut through the trees and passed over a swampy section in the middle of its 200′ length. Fortunately, we had some idea of how to build a durable road from observing the road building of our neighbor, the farmer. He had built several woodland roads and driveways in his time, on different types of soil, and his advice was simple: "Use rock and plenty of it."

When the bulldozer had cleared our lot and was leaving, we had a roadbed made. This was done by digging a channel about 1 foot deep the length of the driveway and about 8 feet wide. We then proceeded to fill it completely with rock. Some areas were so soft that a ½-ton truckload of rock just dissappeared in the mud. When the rocks were in place, we bought some gravel from a contractor and had it dumped in the road. This procedure showed up the faults of our driveway. Several times the large truck wheels would shove aside the rock and sink in the soft soil of the swampy section. This resulted in much clashing of gears, gnashing of teeth, and ripping open of great holes in our so carefully built roadway. But finally the road was in place and we could safely drive over it with our truck.

That winter and following spring the roadbed settled in many places so we covered the entire road once again with a layer of large stones, then gravel. There are still a few low spots waiting for a load of small rocks but the road is now solid throughout even the wettest times, and I no longer have to cross my fingers when a large truck comes to deliver sand or gravel.

If you have an area that has a small brook running across it, or a heavy runoff during a rain, then a culvert will have to be installed in your driveway. This is usually a large pipe laid underneath a road to form a channel for the water to pass through. If you cannot obtain a proper culvert pipe, then you can make one very easily with heavy planking. If treated with a preservative or several

coats of used motor oil, it will last many years (Fig. 2-10).

DIMENSIONS AND DIGGING

The standard method many builders use to lay out the dimensions of the house involves the use of *batter boards,* measuring tape (50-foot), and lines. (Fishing line is excellent for this.)

Batter boards are 1 × 3-inch boards nailed to upright stakes to form a 90° angle at each corner of the house layout. Lines, called *batter lines,* are attached to the boards and extended to outline the places where the footing and walls of the house will be. Using this method, the lines are 1 foot or more above the ground and straight ditches can be dug without disturbing these guidelines. One line can be used to indicate the center of the ditch, or several lines indicating the inside and outside edges of the ditch. A *plumb bob* (a string with a pointed weight on one end) placed at the intersection of two lines will show where the corner of the footing is to be (Figs. 2-11 and 2-12).

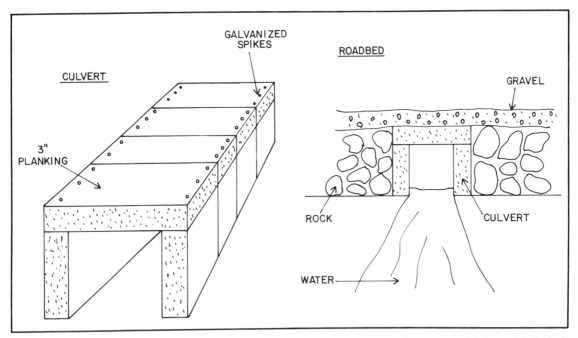

Fig. 2-10. A culvert permits water to flow beneath the roadbed. A culvert can be made with a large metal pipe or 3-inch plank. Paint a wood culvert with several coats of used motor oil or perservative before installation.

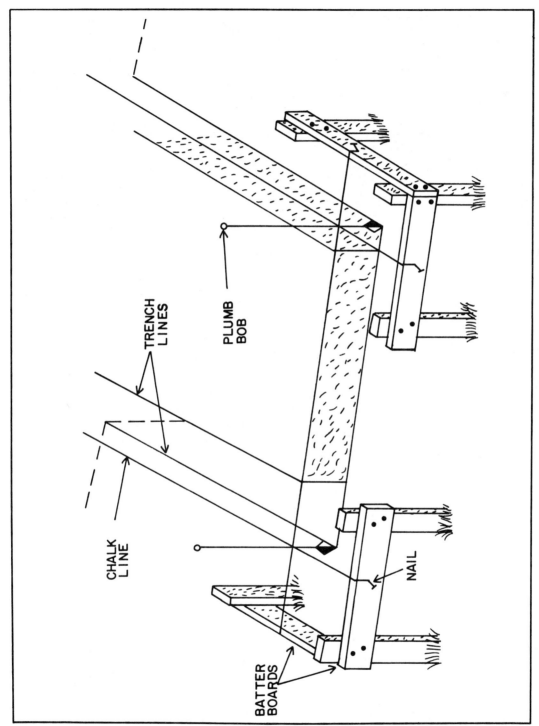

TRENCH LINES

PLUMB BOB

CHALK LINE

NAIL

BATTER BOARDS

Fig. 2-11. To outline the dimensions of a trench, batter boards and lines are used. Lines are attached to boards installed at the four corners of foundation. The trench is dug without disturbing these guidelines.

Fig. 2-12. Placement of forms for wall section.

To make sure that the outlines of your footing are *square* (equal on all sides), the distance from corner to corner (diagonally) is measured. Both diagonals must be equal. The footing must be an exact rectangle and not slanted, which would make building a house on it impossible (Fig. 2-13).

The batter lines must also be perfectly level, enabling you to make the bottom of the trench level and of the required depth. (A 4-foot level is best for this job.) When the batter line is level, a plumb bob is used to measure the distance between the line and the bottom of the trench. Thus, despite uneven ground contours, the top of the footing is easily leveled later on (Fig. 2-14).

Dig around the perimeter of your footing, making sure that the trench is below the frost line. If you encounter bedrock, do your best to clean it of dirt so that it will make a firm bond with the concrete. The concrete will be poured directly into the rectangular trench, so the trench walls should be as

neat as you can make them. If the earth is sandy, the ditch may have to be lined with lumber or some other material to prevent cave-ins. Old wall paneling is good for this. Where it becomes necessary to pour concrete above the trench to retain the level top of the footing, wooden forms are erected along the sides to encase the wet concrete (Fig. 2-15).

STONES, SAND, AND GRAVEL

Prior to the pour you should have ready sand, gravel, water, tools, plus an ample supply of clean stones. These stones should be free of mud, dirt, and any moss because concrete will not bond to a dirty stone. These stones are to be used as *fillers* in the concrete footing and will save you considerable concrete. Use both large and small stones randomly mixed. For our footing we used about four ½-ton truckloads of rock.

There are two procedures from which you can choose. Either mix the concrete by the trench

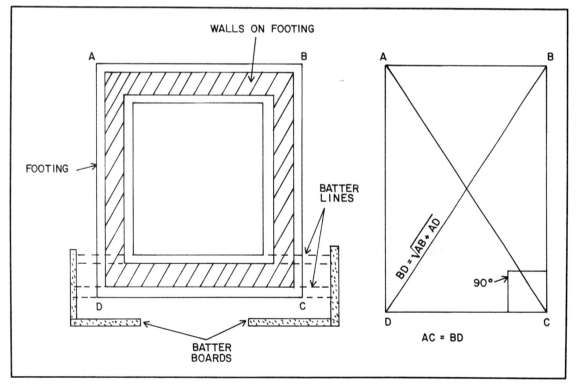

Fig. 2-13. Top view of the walls sitting on the footing as outlined by batter lines. To check that all the corners are equally 90°, diagonal measurements are taken. If they are equal, then the foundation is parallel on all sides and square at the corners.

31

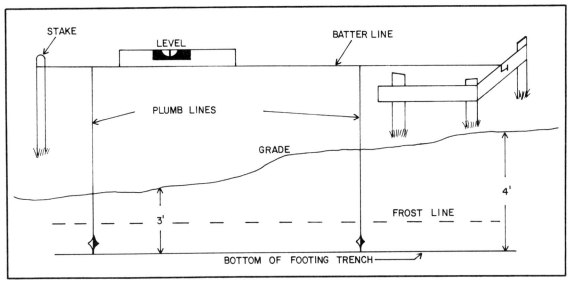

Fig. 2-14. Batter lines ensure even digging, despite uneven ground contours. This keeps the trench bottom below frost line and slope neither up or down. Batter lines are also used to level the top of the footing, using a plumb bob to retain equal measurements between the line and the footing.

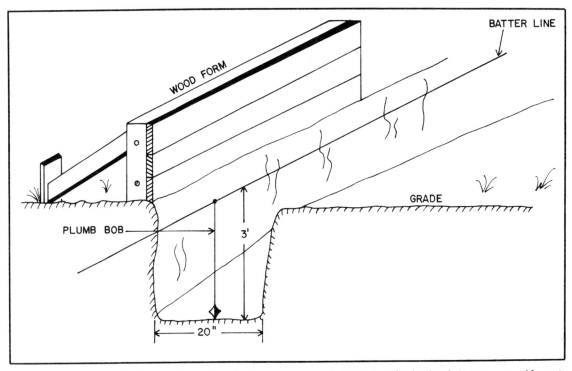

Fig. 2-15. The top of the footing trench may slope due to uneven ground. To keep the footing level at top, use wood forms to encase the wet concrete. They are erected on both sides of the trench and braced in position with 1-inch lumber.

(wheeling the sand and gravel to the mixer) and pour directly into the trench, or locate the mixer by the sand and gravel piles and wheel the concrete to the trench for dumping. Use whichever method is most feasible.

Having all the materials on hand and ready before you begin is a good practice to follow throughout the building process. It assures you that time won't be wasted in the middle of a crucial part of your work by having to run for more cement or stones. The filler stones used for the footing should be unloaded in the center of your house location, inside the footing perimeter. Then, when the footing goes in and the walls go up, it is a simple matter to reach for a stone. Piling them on the outside means more overall distance to carry them. When the walls are up, remaining stones are removed through doorways and used for any number of odd jobs. We used many loads of stone in our driveway and in some drainage ditches that we dug.

To obtain sand and gravel, you can either buy it from a supplier or seek it out in the surrounding area. Perhaps there is someone who has an area of sand or gravel and would sell it reasonably if you did the hauling. If you have sand or gravel on your own property, then your wall costs will be low indeed.

When buying these materials, try to get a local contractor or mason to recommend a supplier of quality sand and gravel. Poor sand and gravel equals poor concrete. The criteria to look for are these: the gravel should not contain large stones (over an average of 1 inch in diameter) but rather should be a mixture of stones from small pebbles to sand. The sand should be fine, free-running, and contain no stones at all. Neither sand nor gravel should contain any clay or loam, roots, grass, or debris. When you buy sand and gravel it is available in two grades, either *pit run* or *screened*. Pit run (or *band run*) means it's dug directly from the ground and delivered to your site. Screened means that all the aforementioned debris has been removed. The latter costs a bit more but is ready for immediate use.

First of all, when obtaining sand, inspect it for obvious debris such as roots and sod. Next, take a handful and squeeze it tightly. If it tends to clump and stay clumped, it has too much clay or loam content.

You can screen sand and gravel yourself. To do so you need only mount a slanted wire screen on a frame and shovel the sand or gravel onto it. The smaller particles pass through to fall into a wheelbarrow and the larger rocks and debris do not. The size of the screen's mesh varies according to your needs. For gravel, the mesh should be anywhere from ¾ to 1 inch and for sand from ⅛ to ¼ inch. The ¼-inch sand screen is suitable for wall concrete, but the ⅛-inch mesh is used to screen sand for use in mortar, described in Chapter 3. Sand from the seashore is of no use since it has too much salt content and will deteriorate concrete.

The cement used is regular portland cement, which is a type of cement and not a brand name. The cement we used is standard construction cement and not the quick-drying type or any other special type of cement. It comes in 1-cubic-foot bags. We bought 10 bags at a time. The reason for this was storage space. Cement must be kept absolutely dry, otherwise it hardens in the bag and you then have 1 cubic foot of expensive rock. We stored our cement in a barn and when on site we covered it with plastic. Thus we used up our cement as we needed it and none was stored for a long period, at risk of becoming damp.

Water for the concrete was not available at our site since we had no well at the time. We brought water to the site in two 45-gallon drums on the back of our truck. We quickly found that it was necessary to cover the open tops of the drums with plastic, tied tightly with rope, in order to arrive with full drums. The water was clean well water, which is best for quality concrete. Dirty or muddy water should not be used if at all possible.

CALCULATIONS

Sand and gravel are sold by the *yard*. This is a cubic yard, which is a volume of sand measuring 3 × 3 × 3-foot equaling 27 cubic feet. When you talk to a supplier of sand and gravel, he will generally ask how many yards you want and tell you his truck sizes. For example, an average dump truck carries a load of approximately 7 yards and a tandem truck carries 11 yards or more.

If you were pouring your footing with solid concrete, determining the amount needed would be simple. Just determine the total cubic footage of your footing in feet (length × width × height) and divide by 27 for the number of yards.

> Example: Your footing is 30 × 20 × 2 feet deep and 20 inches wide.
> Total length: $30 + 30 + 20 + 20 = 100$ feet
> Width: 20 inches = 1 2/3 = foot
> Height: = 2 feet
> Thus, volume = $100 × 1 \, 2/3 × 2 = 333 \, ⅓$ cubic feet.
> 333 ⅓ ÷ 27 = 12.3 yards.

The answer of 12.3 yards is the total amount of sand and gravel needed to fill your trench. But how much of sand and how much of gravel?

To calculate this you must know the mix you will use; the *ratio* of cement, sand, and gravel that forms the concrete blend. The ratios vary according to the use for which the concrete is intended. For example, a footing need not have a smooth surface but must be very strong. A mortar mixed to put bricks together must be smooth and sticky. Each has its own ratio and is expressed using three numbers. Note that 1:2:4 is the mix we used for our footing and means one part cement to two parts sand to four parts gravel. When actually mixing concrete, this would mean one shovelful of cement, two shovelfuls of sand, and four of gravel. In a mixer, a load would be two cement, four sand, and eight gravel.

You could use a mix of 1:6 for a footing: one part cement to six parts gravel, but the addition of the sand makes the concrete smoother and it bonds better to the filler stones. To complete your calculations you must take into account the filler stones. They will occupy about ⅓ to ½ of the volume of the footing, which equals about 5 yards of concrete. This is a considerable saving of sand, gravel, and cement.

Cement, as mentioned, is sold in bags containing 1 cubic foot. To figure out how much you need, using the prior example, the method is as follows:

> Yards for footing = 12.3
> Subtract filler stones: 12.3 − 5 = 7.3 yards
> Mix is 1:2:4
> (1 yard of cement to 6 yards of sand and gravel or 1/6 yard of cement to 1 yard of sand and gravel.)
> Since 1 yard = 3 × 3 × 3 or 27 cubic feet
> Then 1 yard of cement = 27 bags (1/6 yard = 4½ bags)
> Thus, the total for the above is:
> (total sand and gravel) 7.3 yards × 4½ = 32.8 or 33 bags

To calculate the materials for the house walls, the same method is used except the mix is a little different, as discussed in Chapter 3.

There are simple directions for mixing concrete that give excellent and uniform results. First, if using a mixer, mix some water and cement (about ½ to ⅓ gallons of water to two shovelfulls of cement) plus a shovelful of gravel and let it mix. This breaks up any clumps of dry cement and liquifies the whole mass. Next, add the remaining sand and gravel gradually plus additional water to keep the mixture moist. When all the ingredients are in the mixer, it should have the consistency of thick porridge. Be careful adding the water. Too wet a mix and the cement sinks to the bottom of the footing, leaving a flaking and soft top on the footing; too dry and the concrete becomes porous and won't bond well with the filler stones. Finally, be sure and let the concrete mix thoroughly before dumping it.

INSTALLING FORMS

Holes must be built into the footing through which the plumbing will enter and exit. There must be notches made in the top of the footing to accommodate the main beam or beams of the floor structure. Wooden forms are built and installed in the bottom of the trench. Others are attached to the footing forms to accomplish this. Our footing has a notch in

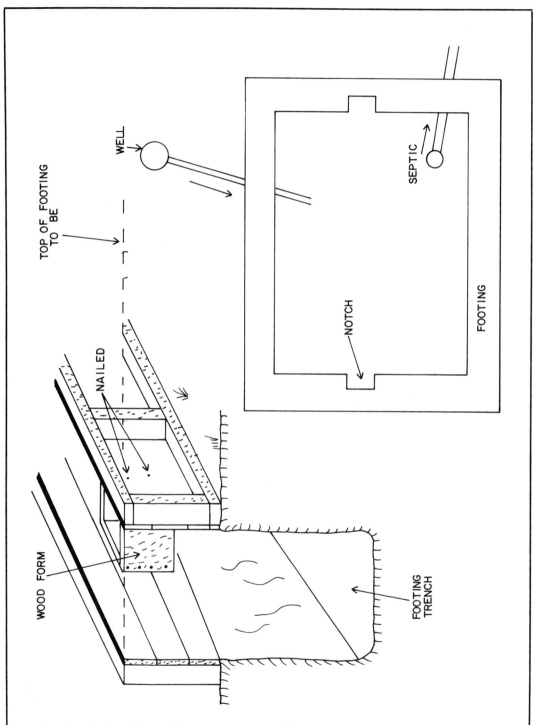

Fig.2-16.Notches in the top of the footing accommodate the main beam.Small wooden forms are placed in the larger forms and surrounded with wet concrete. When later removed, the negative impression left by the form creates the required notch.

35

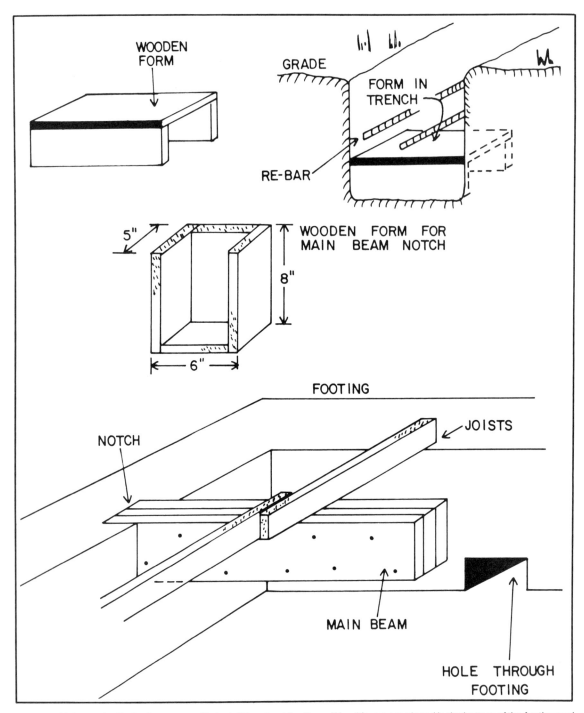

Fig. 2-17. Holes under the footing are used to install the plumbing lines. Wood forms are placed in the bottom of the footing and encased in wet concrete. Rebar is placed above them for strength. Note the floor joists resting on the main beam, which fits in the notch built in the footing.

each of its shorter sides; therefore, the main beam runs parallel to the long dimension of the house. The floor joists rest on the main beam on one end and the footing on the other (Figs. 2-16 and 2-17).

The forms for the plumbing lines are placed in the bottom of the trench, and the concrete is poured directly on top of them. *Rebar* (reinforcing bars) is placed over these forms after a 2 to 3-inch layer of wet concrete is poured. Mark the spot where these forms are so they are easily located when the footing is completed. To install the plumbing later, it is only necessary to dig a trench next to the marked spots to pass underneath the footing.

The forms for the main beam notches are removed when the footing has hardened so be sure that their outside dimensions are accurate; otherwise, the main beam won't fit snugly.

To begin the footing pour a 2- to 3-inch layer of concrete in the footing trench for a distance of about 10 feet. Install rebar and cover it with more concrete, about 2 inches thick. Add some filler stones and press them into the wet concrete, making sure that no stone touches another and each has enough space to be completely encased in concrete. Cover these with concrete and continue the process until the trench is filled to the proper level. During the pour, pieces of ½-inch rebar are bent into 90 degree angles and added to the corners of the footing for added strength. These pieces should project at least 3 feet around each side of the corner.

With the help of my brother, it took us three days to pour the footing. Barbara and I placed the stones while he mixed the concrete. When one day's pour was finished, we slanted the concrete

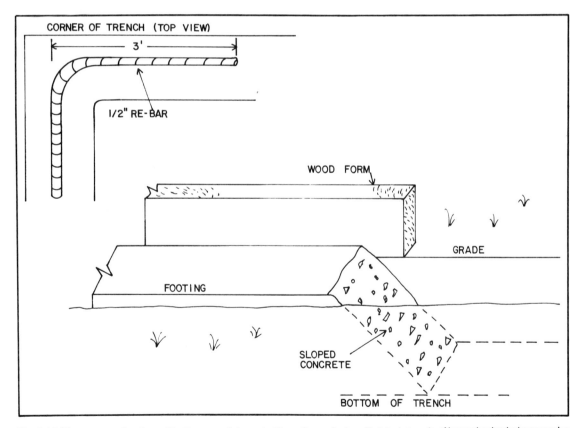

Fig. 2-18. The corners of walls and footing are reinforced with sections of rebar. Twisted strands of heavy barbed wire may also be used. When a section of footing is poured and must be left until the next pour to be completed, it is sloped as shown. This provides a better bond on the next pour and does not create a vertical crack where the two sections join.

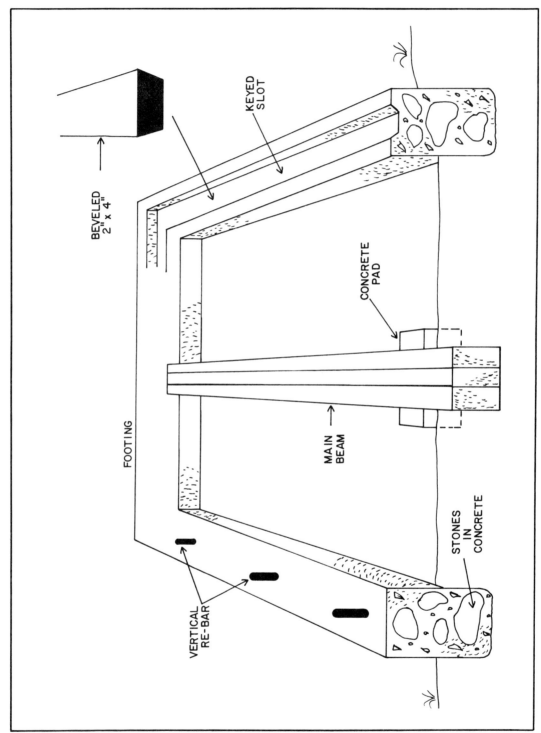

BEVELED
2" x 4"

KEYED
SLOT

FOOTING

CONCRETE
PAD

MAIN
BEAM

VERTICAL
RE-BAR

STONES
IN
CONCRETE

Fig. 2-19. Completed footing showing the main beam and methods of anchoring the walls using vertical rebar or keying, made by inserting a beveled piece of 2 × 4 in wet concrete. When later removed, a slot is left into which the poured concrete walls anchor themselves.

where we ended and left it rough to give an overlapping bond on the next pour (Fig. 2-18).

To finish the top of the footing and level it we used a large trowel and batter lines. It need not be smooth because the roughness will provide a better bond with the first section of stone wall. Short pieces of rebar were placed vertically in the wet concrete sticking up about 6 inches. These anchor the wall later on. Be careful of placement though because you don't want a 6-inch piece of bar protruding where there is no wall.

Another method of anchoring the wall to the footing is by *keying* the top of the footing. A leveled piece of 2 × 4 is embedded in the top of the wet concrete and removed when the footing is dry.

When the wall is poured, the concrete fills the slot and is firmly anchored (Fig. 2-19).

We then covered the wet concrete with used cement bags and a tarpaulin to protect it from the elements and left it for a week to cure. During this time, we poured the concrete pads (about 2 × 2 foot) that would be the supports for the main beam. These pads were spaced approximately 8 feet apart along the line of placement for the future main beam.

The top of each pad stopped at least 10 inches below the top of the footing. This was done to give space to maneuver the main beam later on if it required adjustment either up or down. We then prepared to build the walls.

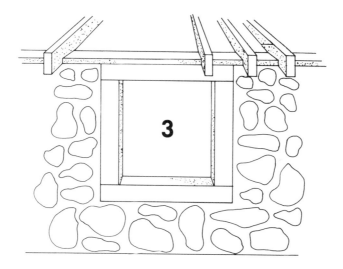

Walls and Windows

HOUSE BUILDING REQUIRES STEP-BY-STEP CON-struction methods. Each stage of building is dependent upon the stage before; therefore, the complete house is designed so that features required in stage nine, for example, are prepared for in stage two. Thus, in building the walls you must allow for simultaneously built design aspects such as windows, which are an integral part of the walls.

Along with designing the locations of window and door openings, you must devise means of fastening the interior wall finishing to the bare concrete of the inside walls. Window frame sizes and the method of installation must also be decided upon. I will deal with each of these considerations in turn.

MATERIALS

Wall building materials include sand, gravel, cement, stone, lumber for window frames and forms, and reinforcing bar.

All the lumber used for our forms, window beams, roof beams, floor joists, and interior walls was obtained by cutting our own logs and having them sawn at a local mill, along with some logs we purchased from a neighbor. It was worth the effort of cutting and buying logs for milling into lumber because it was considerably less expensive than buying from a building supplier. Also, we had some lumber cut to our own specifications, which were not standard lumber dimensions.

Recycled lumber is often readily obtainable. Perhaps you could locate an old building destined to be torn down and buy the lumber for a minimal fee. There are also dealers who sell recycled lumber already cleaned of nails. When buying or salvaging recycled lumber, be sure it is still sound and not cracked or suffering from dry rot. If in doubt, ask a friend, or someone knowledgeable, to inspect it with you. Try to remember that any savings gained are worth a little extra effort.

LUMBER

The types of lumber we used in our house were spruce, pine, hemlock, oak, and maple. The first three are softwoods, the last two are hardwoods. The type of lumber you will use depends upon what is available in your area and the specific use for which you intend it. In our area of Eastern Canada, the species mentioned are common and our woodlot contains specimens of each. On the west coast of the United States and Canada, fir and redwood are among the most common types used for building.

Lumber is divided into catagories and grades by building suppliers. The basic catagories are *rough lumber* and *finished lumber*, with grades for each. Lumber, when just sawn from a tree, is rough surfaced and each board is not exactly the same thickness, width, or length. To produce a smooth surface, the lumber is planed, which also makes each board the same thickness. Lumber can be planed on one side, two sides, and on its edges—all four sides. Each type is available from a dealer and you must specify what you require.

For boarding in the outside walls of a wood frame house, or for a sub-floor or roof, it is not necessary to have lumber planed on four sides. If it is planed on one side only, all the boards will be of uniform thickness (which eliminates one board sticking up above the rest—an undesirable feature in a floor or roof). This is termed *dressed one side* (DIS).

The boards that you use to trim the outside of the house should be planed on all four sides (D4S). It makes them easier to paint, better to look at, and easier to fit for tight joints. Boards used inside the house are also planed on four sides, and they have their edges specially cut to make tight joints (described in Chapter 5). *Boards* are generally 1-inch or less in thickness and of any length and width. When the lumber exceeds 1 inch in thickness it becomes a plank, generally 2 to 3 inches thick and is designated by its dimensions. Lumber over this thickness is called a *timber* or *beam*. Thus, 2×8 means a plank 2 inches thick and 8 inches wide. It is usually planed on all four sides. Some standard lumber sizes are: boards—1×2, 1×3, 1×5, etc; planks—2×4, 2×6, 2×8, etc; beams—6×6, 6×8, 8×8, and so on.

Our floor was made using 2×8-inch floor joists resting on a 6×8-inch main beam and cov-

ered with 1-inch boards of varying widths and lengths. Each plank has a specific strength related to its thickness. A board or plank placed edgewise between two supports will bear more weight without bending than if laid flat. Thus the planks used to support a floor or a roof are installed edgewise and spaced equal distances apart. The amount of weight each size of lumber will support without appreciable bending depends upon the type of wood and the distance it has to reach, its *span*. Planks are placed side to side to support a floor, and the distance between each is measured from *center to center*. The closer together they are the more weight they can carry; similarly the shorter their span the greater their load-bearing capacity (Fig. 3-1).

When you design your floor and roof, these factors are taken into account and your plans made accordingly. There are specific tables that indicate the proper size lumber to use for designated spans and applied loads. These tables are meant as general guidelines only and will vary depending on your application. For example, if you plan to put a 400-pound stove in one area and sit it on 800 pounds of stone hearth, you will obviously have to reinforce that area of the floor. Our plans were to build as solidly as possible from footing to roof, thus we used 2×8-inch floor joists on 16-inch centers with a

Table 3-1. Floor Joist Table.

FLOOR JOIST	SPACED APART	SPAN
2" X 6"	14"	8'
2" X 6"	16"	9'
2" X 8"	14"	13'
2" X 8"	16"	12'
2" X 8"	24"	10'
2" X 10"	14"	16'
2" X 10"	16"	15'

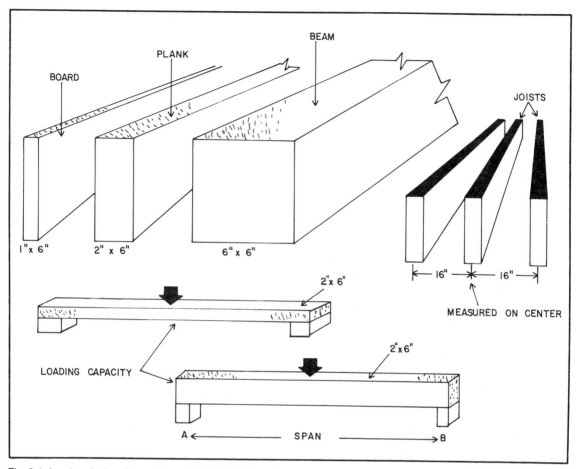

Fig. 3-1. Lumber designations. A board is 1-inch thick, a plank 2 or 3 inches thick. Above these thicknesses are timbers or beams. The strength of a board or plank is much greater when on edge. This loading capacity depends upon the size of the lumber and the distance it has to reach, called its span. When lumber is placed on edge the distance between each board is measured from the center of one to the center of the other and is termed *measuring on center*.

span of 9 feet (Table 3-1).

Lumber is measured either by the *board foot* or by the *linear foot*, sometimes called a *running foot*. The dimensions of the lumber are used differently for each method. It can all be very confusing if you go unprepared to a lumber dealer and ask for some boards. He will ask you "What size and how many feet do you want? Dressed one side or four? Any specific lengths?"

Board feet are calculated as follows:

1 b.f. (board foot) = a piece of wood 1-inch thick × 1-foot long × 1-foot wide.

Thus, board feet = length (feet) × width (feet) × thickness (inches)

Example: a board 12 feet long × 6 inches wide × 1 inch thick.

$$b.f. = 1 \times w \times t = 12 \times 6/12 \times 1 = 6 \, b.f.$$

Example #2. A board 12 feet long × 8 inches wide × 2 inches thick.

$$b.f. = 12 \times 8/12 \times 2 = 16 \, b.f.$$

Using this method, you can convert from board feet directly to square feet. For example, if your floor is 20 feet wide and 30 feet long:

Area of floor 20 × 30 = 600 square feet.

A b.f. is 1-foot × 1-foot × 1-inch, which is 1 square foot of lumber 1 inch thick. Therefore, if you use 1-inch boards to cover the floor, you will need 600 b.f. of lumber. Cost estimates are then easily done. Lumber is generally priced per 1000 b.f. If, for example, 1000 b.f. of 1-inch boards cost $300, then for the above floor the price is:

$$1000 \text{ b.f.} = \$300 \quad 100 \text{ b.f.} = \$30 \quad 600 \text{ b.f.} = \\ 30 \times 6 = \$180$$

You could order 600 b.f. of 1-inch lumber from a supplier for $180 and have enough to cover your floor. (Almost.) There will be wastage due to cutting the boards to fit the floor joists. To compensate for this, an order of 700 b.f. would be more practical.

Linear or running feet means the exact length of the lumber, measured in feet. If you wish to buy three pieces of 2 × 8, each 10 feet long, then the total is 3 × 10 = 30 linear feet. Pricing by this method is listed according to the dimensions of the lumber. For example 2 × 4 at 10¢ per foot, 2 × 8 at 30¢ per foot, and so on. You specify the total amount of linear feet you want of a certain dimension and pay accordingly. Whereas b.f. measurement is helpful when estimating area coverage, linear measurement is useful when you want a certain sized lumber for a specific use, such as building a set of wooden steps or erecting studding.

A final aspect concerning lumber is whether it is *air dried* or *kiln dried*. Air dried lumber is stored either in a building or outdoors. Kiln dried refers to lumber dried in a large oven. Both methods remove moisture from freshly cut lumber, called *green lumber*. Green lumber, if you use it to build with, will very often shrink, warp, twist, and crack after it is in place. This is obviously undesirable because it will destroy your carefully fitted woodworking. To avoid this, lumber should be air dried before you buy it. (If you have logs sawn, as we did, you must store the lumber under cover for at least six to eight months.) Air drying removes enough moisture to make the lumber suitable for general house building, but if you need very dry lumber, for building cabinets or furniture, then kiln dried is best. The oven heat dries the lumber more thoroughly than the air, and as a result it will not dry out any more after you use it—the cause of warping, twisting, and cracking. Kiln dried is usually much more expensive than air dried, and it does have one aspect of which you should be aware. It cannot be exposed to moisture. If you bought kiln dried lumber and stored it in a basement or an outdoor shed, it would very likely warp because it absorbs moisture from the air because it is so dry. Kiln dried lumber should be used in a heated area. Preferably, any furniture or cabinets should be built on site at their destined locations.

CONCRETE AND STONE

The estimates for cement, sand, and gravel for the walls are the same as for the footing. The volume of wall is calculated by multiplying the length × width × thickness in feet and then subtracting the areas for the doors and windows (Fig. 3-2). The height of our wall was 9 feet from footing to wall top. We chose this height because the floor would take 1 foot from this height, leaving 8 feet as an ample interior wall height. Also, 9 feet takes exactly six levels of stonework as measured by the 18-inch high wooden forms we used.

The percentage of stone to concrete in the walls was approximately 50 percent, and the average weight of stone and concrete is 150 pounds per cubic foot. The total weight of our stone walls is in the vicinity of 50 tons. Add the weight of the roof, floor, and other wood, plus furnishings, and the necessity for a solid foundation becomes obvious.

SLIPFORMS

The method we used for erecting the stone walls originated, as far as we can determine, with Ernest Flagg, an American architect, and is termed the *Flagg slipform method*. His method originally in-

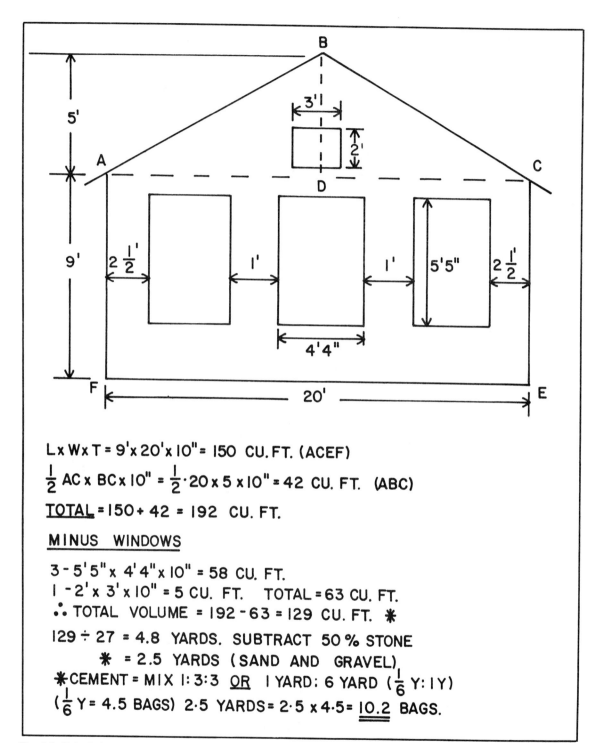

$L \times W \times T = 9' \times 20' \times 10'' = 150$ CU. FT. (ACEF)

$\frac{1}{2} AC \times BC \times 10'' = \frac{1}{2} \cdot 20 \times 5 \times 10'' = 42$ CU. FT. (ABC)

<u>TOTAL</u> $= 150 + 42 = 192$ CU. FT.

<u>MINUS WINDOWS</u>

$3 - 5'5'' \times 4'4'' \times 10'' = 58$ CU. FT.
$1 - 2' \times 3' \times 10'' = 5$ CU. FT. TOTAL $= 63$ CU. FT.
∴ TOTAL VOLUME $= 192 - 63 = 129$ CU. FT. ✱

$129 \div 27 = 4.8$ YARDS. SUBTRACT 50% STONE
  ✱ $= 2.5$ YARDS (SAND AND GRAVEL)
✱CEMENT $=$ MIX $1:3:3$ <u>OR</u> 1 YARD: 6 YARD ($\frac{1}{6}$ Y: 1Y)
($\frac{1}{6}$ Y $= 4.5$ BAGS) 2.5 YARDS $= 2.5 \times 4.5 = \underline{10.2}$ BAGS.

Fig. 3-2. Calculations to figure volume of house.

volved the use of heavy wooden forms which, although portable, were cumbersome. His basic technique, however, is the one we employed, with some initial modifications to make the forms lighter. As we proceeded, we also gained by experience some ideas and techniques of our own, as no doubt you will also.

Of the many methods of building stone walls, the slipform method is probably the easiest for novices to master. It does not involve any splitting or shaping of stones and the techniques, although simple, produce stone walls that are even, straight, and plumb. When the pointing is done, the walls are comparable in beauty and durability to any that have been professionally built.

The method of laying up a stone wall freehand, either with or without mortar, calls for a good deal of experience, even though it may look easy. We personally know of an instance where a beginner attempted to lay a stone foundation freehand. After much expenditure of labor, it collapsed. Thus a hopeful builder was thoroughly discouraged and perhaps won't try stonework again.

Stone masonry is a profession that in times past was raised to the level of a fine art. Many of the beautiful stone buildings we see still standing are testimony to this. There are masons today who are skilled in the old methods of stone work, but not many of us are willing, or even able, to take the necessary time to practice and acquire the intimate knowledge of stone that is required to be a successful stone mason.

The slipform method possesses features that enable beginners to erect excellent stone walls in a relatively short period of time. It reduces the chances of error to a minimum, and the skills required are easily and quickly learned. Success is ensured if you take your time, are careful, and check each measurement twice.

The basic principle uses portable wooden

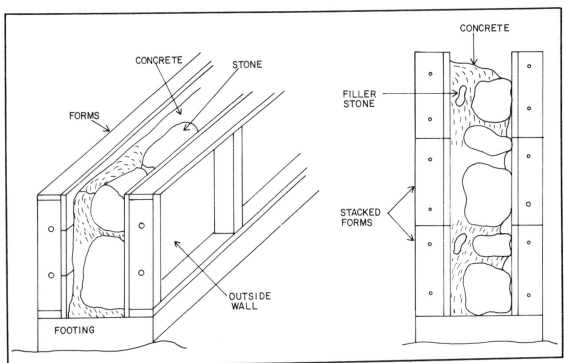

Fig. 3-3. The basic techniqe of slipforming. Stone and concrete is placed between two wooden forms with the stone resting against one of the forms. When the concrete hardens, more forms are stacked on top of the first. More stone and concrete is added, continuing to the top in leapfrog fashion. When forms are removed, the stones form the outside wall face. The inside walls are solid concrete.

Fig. 3-4. Wall forms near top of wall. Note door frame on right.

forms approximately 8 feet long by 1½ feet high erected facing each other about 10 inches apart. (The thickness chosen for the walls.) Into these forms, stones and concrete are placed so that after the concrete hardens and the forms are removed, you have a wall with an outer facing of stone and an inner facing of solid concrete. The forms are then reset to a higher level, the next mixture of stones and concrete is added, and so on until a wall of the desired height is built (Fig. 3-3).

The forms should be built well in advance of any concrete (Fig. 3-4). Thus you not only get a better grasp of the mechanics involved in slipforms, but you have all materials on hand and ready prior to any construction. (We used our forms in the framing of the footing and saved a lot of time by not having to build elaborate form work and then tear it apart.)

ASSEMBLY

The forms were built 8 feet long and 1½ inches high

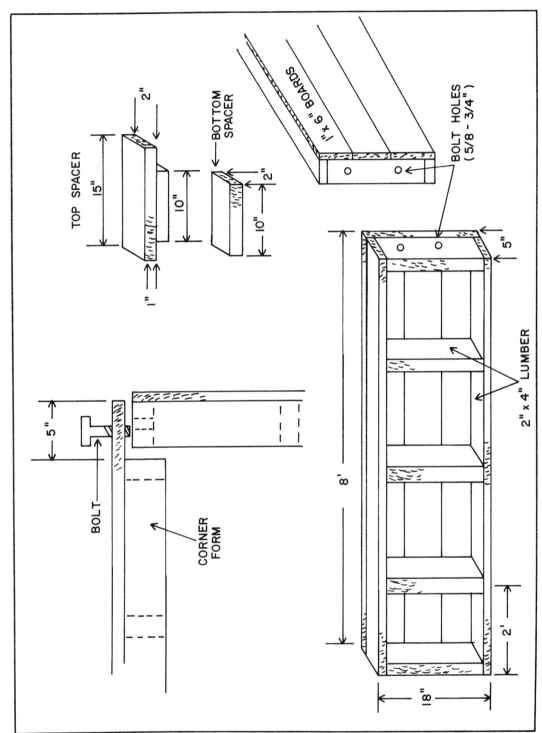

Fig. 3-5. Building the basic slipform. 2 × 4 and 1 × 6 boads are assembled as shown. Special corner forms are built with a projecting lip on one end to facilitate joining when forming a 90° corner. Spacers are used to keep the forms the required distance apart.

TOP SPACER

2"

15"

1"

BOTTOM SPACER

2"

10"

10"

1 × 6 " BOARDS

BOLT HOLES (5/8 - 3/4")

BOLT

CORNER FORM

5"

2" x 4" LUMBER

8'

2'

18"

5"

for convenience. Any longer gives additional weight, and higher forms become awkward to fill. Nevertheless, 10 × 2 foot forms could be used if you desired. We also built several 4 × 1½-foot forms and a few 2 × 1½-foot. In total we built 12 of the 8 × 1½-foot forms, 6 of the 4 × 1½-foot forms, and 4 of the 2 × 1½-foot forms. These forms are still usable and we keep them so by applying a coat of used motor oil over them from time to time.

When not in use, we store them flat and keep them protected from the weather.

To build these forms, we used 2 × 4-inch lumber and 1 × 6-inch boards. To build each form, cut two pieces of 2 × 4 each 8 feet long, five pieces of 2 × 4 each 14 inches long, and three pieces of 1 × 6 boards each 8 feet long. These are assembled as shown in Fig. 3-5. Then ⅝-inch holes are drilled in the end 2 × 4's through which bolts will be fastened.

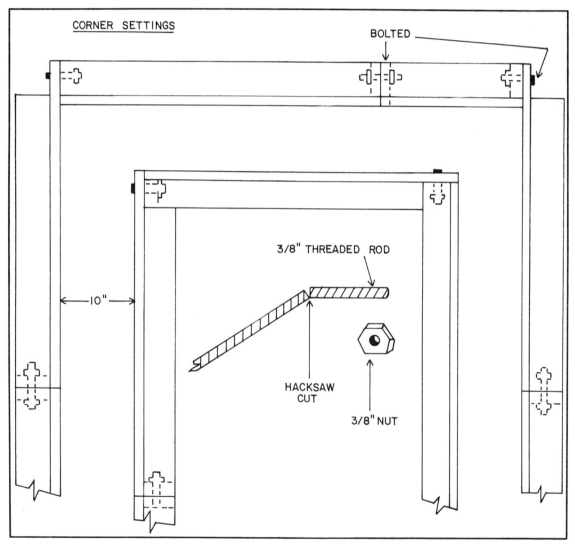

Fig. 3-6. Forms set up for corner settings, bolted in place using ⅜-inch bolts. Bolts may be made using threaded rod and cutting it to bolt length with a hacksaw.

Two forms can then be anchored together horizontally to produce a continuous form of 16 feet or longer where needed. The 4-foot forms are built in the same fashion. (Plywood can be used instead of the 1 × 6 boards.)

We also built four forms with a projecting "lip" on one end. These forms are used for corner settings. The 1 × 6 boards are still 8 feet long, but the 2 × 4 on one end is moved 5 inches toward the center. Bolt holes are drilled in the lip to match those in the ends of the other forms (Fig. 3-6).

Instead of buying a number of expensive ⅜-inch bolts, you can make your own by purchasing lengths of ⅜-inch threaded rod and cutting them in bolt sizes with a hacksaw. Each bolt should be about 6 or 7 inches long and have a nut and washer on each end. We kept our bolts in a can of motor oil to prevent them from rusting and becoming difficult to use.

The thickness of our walls is 10 inches. This size is suitable for a structure with walls rising to 9 feet, but for walls above this height the initial thickness should be increased to 12 or 14 inches. Anything less than 10 inches is not suitable because it will not be sound enough to safely support a roof. Since our footing was 20 inches wide, this left 5 inches on either side of the wall to support the first level of forms.

To place the forms, first choose a section of wall to be built. For example, begin at one corner and extend 16 feet on one side and 8 to 16 feet on the other. By including at least one corner in your first pour, the resulting walls will be self supportive. The walls should be built so that one complete

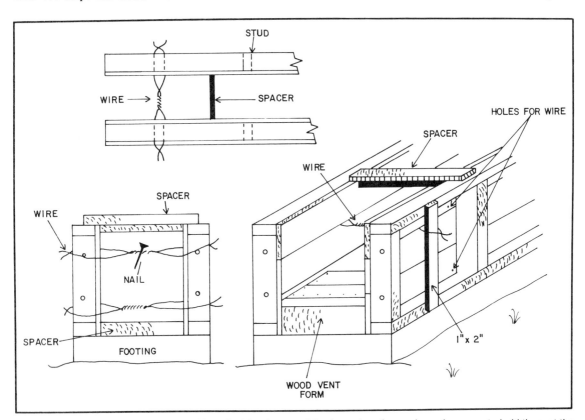

Fig. 3-7. Fastening the forms together with malleable wire to pull the forms together and wood spacers to hold them at the correct wall thickness. Wires are passed through one form, across the intervening space, and around the opposite form before returning to the first form. The wire is then twisted inside the forms, using a 3-inch nail. Note the small wooden form used to create a vent in the lower wall.

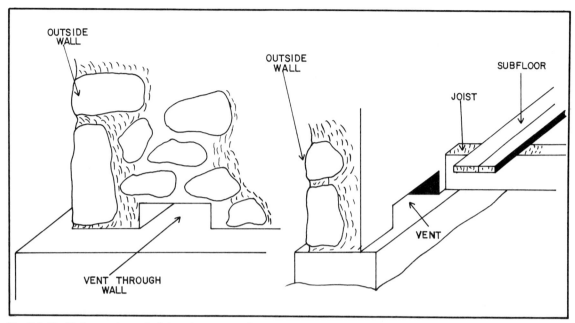

Fig. 3-8. Ventilation vents are built into the stone walls to prevent rotting of the floor joists and beams from dampness. The vents are closed in the winter when the crawl space is warmed by the heating system.

circumference of the house is finished before adding the next level. If one wall is built to 9 feet before the others, it can cause uneven settling and cracking. We found that filling a total of 24 to 32 feet of form was an average day's work, or *pour*, as it is termed.

The forms are secured in place by passing wire through one form, across the 10-inch wall space, through and around the opposite form, and back again, where the two ends are twisted together. The malleable wire should be wrapped around the vertical 2 × 4 of the forms but if they don't line up, a piece of wood can be substituted. A nail is used to twist the wires inside the forms, causing them to tighten and draw the two forms together. Wooden spacers, 10 inches long, are used to keep the forms apart top and bottom (Fig. 3-7). The forms are now quite rigid and only have to be checked with a level to ensure they are 90 degrees vertical and level horizontally. Straight, plumb (vertically straight) walls begin with the first pour and every effort should be made, starting with the footing, to keep each stage as level and straight as possible.

VENTILATION

Next consult your plans. Is there a door frame to install? Are there any openings in the wall that must be prepared for? If you are going to build a wooden floor, it will be necessary to have the crawl space ventilated to prevent condensation and rot. To do so, vent holes are built into the walls just above the footing about 15 inches wide and 5 inches high. Choose vent locations from your plans and build them by putting pre-built wooden forms into place at the bottom of the wall forms and resting on the footing. When the wall is poured and the forms removed, you will then have a vent in the lower wall (Fig. 3-8). These vents can be closed in winter and opened in the summer. They should be screened to prevent entry of insects and flies. The vents open beneath the floor on the inside of the house. By using two or three vents strategically placed you will create a cross flow of air under the floor to effectively prevent rot. (Rebar is put in the wet concrete above these openings for strength, as is done for all wall openings.)

Another venting system was built into the

stone walls to provide fresh air and cool the house in summer. Our large windows couldn't be opened, so a method providing a cooling air flow had to be devised. Since the interior of the house is relatively open, this was easy to do.

The method uses the principle that hot air rises and is replaced by cooler air that rushes in from below. The south side of the house is in the sun and is therefore hotter than the shaded north side. By installing two vents in the lower part of the north wall and one large vent in the upper part of the south wall, an air flow was initiated from cooler to hotter air with the pathway through the long axis of the house.

The north vents were each built 1-foot square and installed about 1½ feet above the floor. One vent is in the bedroom and the other in the bathroom (Fig. 1-7—north wall perspective.) These vents can be opened or closed on the inside of the house and also adjusted to permit a lesser or greater amount of airflow. In the winter, they are sealed on the outside.

The vent on the south side is a 2 × 3-foot window that can also be opened or closed on the inside (Fig. 1-8). The window is near the peak and the area of the window, 6 square feet, is three times that of the 2-foot-square inlet vents. The ratio is thus 3:1 for the hot/cold vents although 2:1 is adequate. The hot vent is always the larger.

Forms were made for the vents in the north wall and installed prior to the pour, whereas the window in the south wall was installed following the methods used for the windows. This cooling system works very well and provides a cool flow of air even during the dog days of summer when the temperature hovers around 90° and the blue haze holds the outside air still (Fig. 3-9).

DOOR AND WINDOW FRAMES

Door and window frames were built of 6 × 6-inch pine beams. We chose this size because they complement the appearance of a stone house and are very strong. You can, however, use conventional

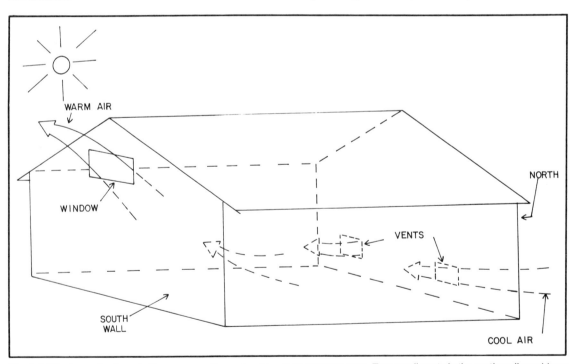

Fig. 3-9. The house is air cooled in summer with a cross flow of air through vents. Two small vents in the north wall provide an intake of air from low down on the wall. Air flows through the house and exits via one larger window higher up in the south wall.

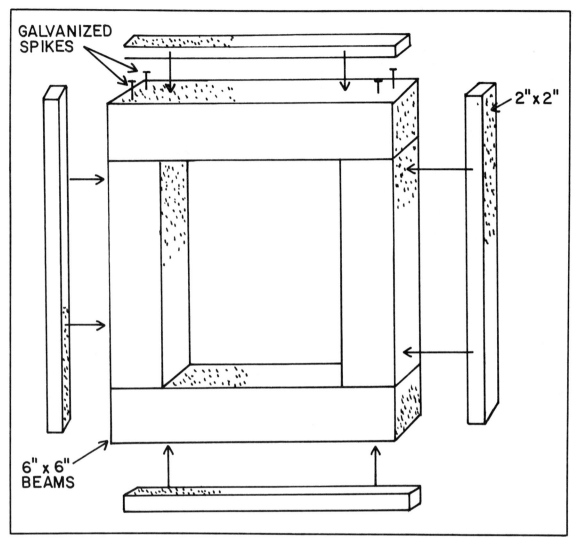

GALVANIZED SPIKES

2" x 2"

6" x 6" BEAMS

Fig. 3-10. The window frames were made using 6 × 6 beams assembled as shown. Two-by-two lumber was fastened around the perimeter of the large frame for extra strength and as a means of preventing drafts when installed. The 2 × 2 acts as a bridge between the large frame and the concrete walls.

window framing of 2 × 6-inch or 2 × 8-inch lumber if it suits your plans.

Our window frames were simply and easily built. After determining the size of our windows, we cut the beams with a small buck saw and assembled them as in Fig. 3-10. The top beam sits squarely on the others without a 45° cut and is quite solid. Ten-inch spikes fastened them together. Next, pieces of 2×2-inch lumber were nailed

around the outer perimeter of the frame as shown. These pieces help to hold the frame securely together and also bridge any gaps between the frame and the concrete. This ensures a good anchoring of the frame in the wall and also stops any drafts.

The frames should be given one or two good coats of a preservative before they are installed in the walls. This will protect them from rotting due to moisture between the frame and concrete. Be careful in your choice of a preservative. Wood preservatives are basically very potent and effective pesticides. They last for years and thus offer a long period of toxicity. It is now believed that sufficient exposure to these chemicals can lead to cancer, tumors, and birth defects. Therefore, if you plan to use these chemicals, wear gloves when using them, use them only outdoors, and don't use them for a greenhouse or on any area near food. A good substitute for the protection of the frames where they

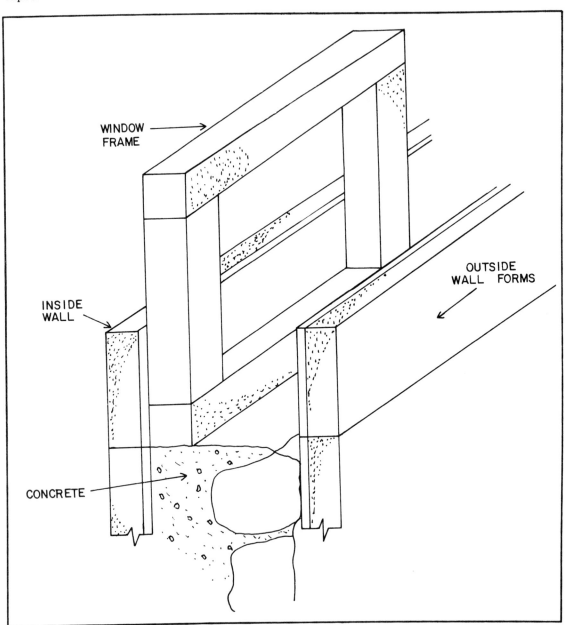

WINDOW FRAME

OUTSIDE WALL FORMS

INSIDE WALL

CONCRETE

Fig. 3-11. Placement of the window frame in the forms. It rests firmly against the inside wall form and is braced in place. When the walls are finished, the frame will be 4 inches from the outside wall face.

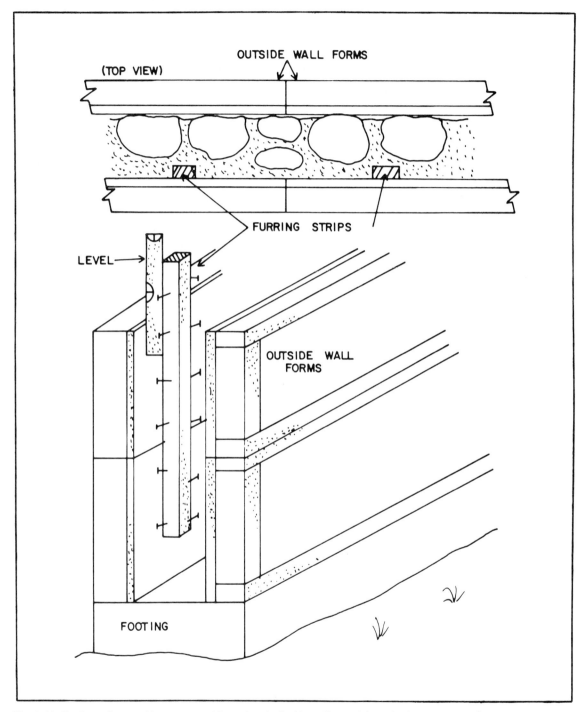

Fig. 3-12. Furring strips provide a means of fastening the inside wall materials to the bare concrete. Two-by-two pieces of lumber are studded with nails and inset in the wet concrete. They are fastened to the inside wall forms, leveled and plumbed before being encased in concrete.

meet the concrete is used motor oil. Brush on two or three coats of the oil and let it sink in before installing the frames (Fig. 3-11).

The door frames were built with 6 × 6 beams in the same manner as the window frames. The outside dimensions were 4 × 7 feet giving a door size of 3 × 6 feet.

FURRING STRIPS

In order to be able to finish the inside wall, which will be smooth concrete, there must be some means of fastening lumber to it. This can be done with special masonry glues but it is messy, expensive, and difficult, especially if the concrete surface is uneven. The best method is the use of *furring strips*.

These are pieces of 2 × 2-inch lumber of various lengths imbedded in the concrete to provide solid wood in which to nail.

To make them, cut a piece of 2 × 2 lumber about 3 feet long and drive old nails into two opposite sides. This piece is then set vertically in the wall forms against the inside form and fastened there. It should be plumbed so as not to hamper successive levels of wall by protruding beyond the wall face. The concrete is poured around the strips and held there by the nails. When the forms are removed there is a smooth concrete wall with a series of vertical wood strips in which to nail. The furring strips should extend the full height of the walls and be spaced about 4 feet apart around the

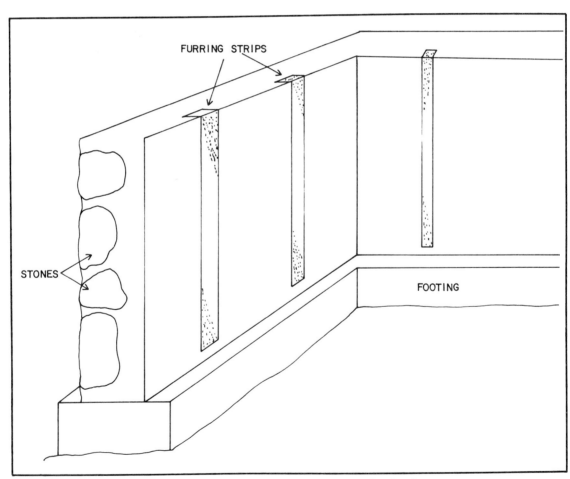

Fig. 3-13. A diagram showing the appearance of the furring strips in the completed wall.

wall. They must not project above the final wall height or into a window space (Figs. 3-12 and 3-13).

BUILDING WALLS

The technique for the placing of stones and pouring of concrete is very simple. Yet without some planning and a few basic principles, you may encounter unnecessary difficulties.

In choosing stone for your house, make sure that they are clean. They should have no mud or dirt caked on them nor any moss. (Stones with a little moss can be cleaned with a stiff wire brush.) It is simply too laborious to try and clean dirty stones. It is easier to spend the time locating suitable stone exposed in fields and ditches. Best of all are old stone piles that farmers created while clearing fields. One of the farmers who gave us free access to his old stone piles was amused to think that his many long hours spent clearing his fields of useless rock were now contributing to the building of a house. He even showed us piles of stone that were hidden by trees that had grown up over the 30 years since he had placed the stones there.

Stones should ideally be gathered and sorted long before any construction begins. We used stones with one flat face for the wall stone and with two flat faces about 90° apart for cornerstones. We had small stones of all shapes to use as fillers plus several large stones weighing about 200 pounds or so. These large stones were placed in the bottom layers of the wall, not only because they are too heavy to lift very high but, because larger stones should be placed near the bottom for the best visual effect. By using large stones near the bottom and reducing the average size of the stones as you build higher, you achieve a look of solidity in the wall. It appears to be resting firmly on the ground. It was for this reason that the Greeks tapered the massive pillars they used in building their temples.

Stones containing iron should be avoided because they will rust, causing long, ugly brown streaks to run down your carefully built stonework. These streaks are nearly impossible to remove. You will soon recognize a stone containing iron. If in doubt, break the stone with a hammer and iron rust will appear on the inside.

We used mainly granite plus a few other types of stone, such as quartz, for varying effects. We can still look at certain stones and remember the place we found them and sometimes what the weather had been that day.

The type of stone you use for your walls depends upon what is available in your area. In general, almost any type of stone will do providing it doesn't absorb water or crack easily. Angular stone is preferable to round stone because it is easier to fit against the forms if the stones have at least one flat surface. If you choose stones that exhibit lines or grooves on the surface due to layering of the rock, place them so the lines are vertical in the walls, thereby shedding water more readily.

When placing a stone against a form, try to arrange any sloping surface to slant towards the exterior of the wall so that moisture will not be directed inwards. When arranging stones in a line, try to vary their sizes so their appearance avoids clusters of big and small stones. Build as bricklayers do, with a stone above bridging the gap between two stones below.

None of the stones we used were allowed to reach through to the inner wall. They all had an average thickness of 8 inches or less in order to provide a solid thickness of 2 inches concrete on the inside wall. This acts as a barrier to any wind or rain that might find a crack through the stone facing (Fig. 3-14).

Don't use any of those tempting flat stones that are about 2 to 3 inches thick. They don't adhere well to the concrete and will often fall off the wall face, leaving glaring concrete patches. Round stones, such as beach stones, are also very difficult to use because they have no corners or angles for the concrete to grip. You will very quickly develop a feel for stone, and your placement of each one will be quick and sure.

The concrete mixture is also a matter for care. It should not be too dry as it will not grip the stones tightly and result in a leaky wall. Too wet, and the concrete will run between the stone face and the outer form, giving the appearance of a concrete wall with a few stones peeking out here and there. You will gain experience with concrete when you mix it

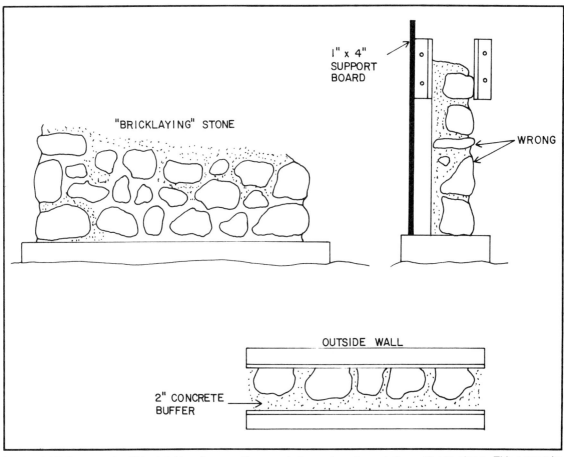

Fig. 3-14. Wall stones should be *bricklayed*—cover the gaps between two stones below with one above. This cannot be precisely done, but it can be approximated. Stones should never project completely through the wall and the tops of each stone should be level or slope toward the outside wall to prevent water from being directed inward. There should also be a 2-inch concrete buffer between stones and inside form.

for the footing, so details picked up will help now.

The basic mix we used for the walls was 1:3:3. One shovelful of cement to three of sand and three of gravel. Our sand and gravel were both free of clay or loam and did not need to be screened. The amount of water to add varies and will come with experience. After a day of rain, for example, we would add less water to the mix because of the damp sand. The appearance of the wet concrete should be like thick oatmeal porridge and uniform in texture. Follow the rules for mixing concrete that were given for the footing. After dumping the concrete into a wheelbarrow, add some water to the mixer to keep it wet and prevent any cement from drying to the sides.

We wheeled the concrete to the forms and used it as needed. As the levels became higher we put the concrete in buckets and carried it up a stepladder to the staging. When carrying a full bucket of concrete up a stepladder, make certain that all of the ladder's four legs are on the ground, otherwise you will be performing some hair-raising balancing and juggling acts.

To begin, place a layer of wet concrete about 2 inches thick in the bottom of the forms. Into this layer of concrete, insert any door frames that will

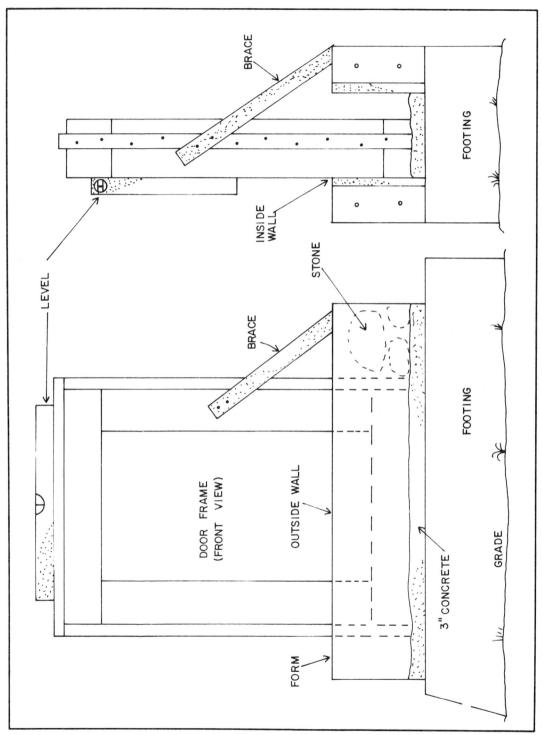

Fig. 3-15. Door frames are built using the same methods as for the windows. They are installed against the inside form and set on 3 inches of wet concrete. Before they are encased in concrete they are leveled, plumbed, and braced. In this instance, the door frame is set directly on the footing.

be sitting directly on the footing. The frame will rest snug against the inside wall form and, since the frames are 6 inches thick, the 4-inch gap between the frame and outside wall form must be bridged with a piece of 2 × 4. Thus, when the wall is finished, the door frame will be inset 4 inches from the outside wall face. (The window frames are installed in the same way except at a higher level in the wall.) The frame is braced in place with 1 × 3-inch lumber and leveled and plumbed before proceeding (Fig. 3-15).

Next, choose a stone and wet it with a sponge dipped in a bucket of water. This wetting provides a better bond with the concrete. The stone is then placed with its best face against the outside form and pushed into the sticky concrete. Continue like this until you have a line of stones about 4 or 5 feet long, or until reaching a window frame, corner, etc. Then fill in behind the stones with more concrete, making sure no stone projects through the wall and that you have maintained a 2-inch barrier of concrete on the inside wall. The concrete is pushed in, under, and around each face stone to hold it as well as possible. Add some filler stones to the spaces behind stones to save on concrete but make sure that no stone touches any other. When the concrete reaches the top of the face stones, add another 2-inch layer over the top and place more face stones until the form is filled.

Ensure that no concrete is squeezed out between the face stones and the outside forms, and don't forget to remove the wooden spacers as you go.

To finish off a form, cover the stones with a thin layer of concrete and slope it toward the outside form (Fig. 3-3). The next pour will then be on top of this day's finished one. Avoid letting any stone protrude above the form because it will often cause the misalignment of the next form if the stone has an edge that juts out beyond the face of the wall. It would then have to be chipped off and the hammer blows could weaken the wall.

When the forms are finished for the day, the wet concrete is covered with empty bags or canvas to protect it from the sun and rain. Concrete must be allowed to cure as it dries so it retains its strength. Forms should not be removed for at least 48 hours and then carefully so you don't smash chunks of semidry concrete out of the wall. This is why a number of forms are handy, since you can proceed with building between pours without disturbing the previous levels.

Thus you proceed in stages around your house, erecting the walls simultaneously on all sides. When one pour is complete, set your next line of forms on top of the finished ones and plumb them. (Forms become self-supportive when the concrete hardens because the binding wires are gripped tightly in the wall. The wires are left imbedded in the wall and the protruding ends are snipped off with wire cutters after the forms are removed.) Level them and proceed to fill them with stones and concrete. To remove the bottom forms, cut the wires and ease them away from the wall. Next, go over the wall with hammer and chisel or a mason's hammer and chip off any lumps or flakes of concrete that are sticking to the stones. Remove any concrete that sticks out beyond the wall face. It is much easier to remove the semidry concrete now than later, when it becomes very hard.

The corners of the walls require special attention. To ensure their solidity and prevent cracking, ½-inch rebar is inserted in the wet concrete as shown in Fig. 3-16. The rebar is cut about 5 to 6 feet long and given a 90° bend. It is installed about every foot, vertically, in the wall. (We have used double stranded barbed wire in place of rebar for the wall corners. We cut a section of wire about 12 feet long, folded it in half, and twisted it together to give a solid 6-foot piece of wire. We then bent this in two to form a 90° angle and inserted it in the wall.) Rebar is also placed above openings for windows, doors, and vents and should protrude about 1 to 2 feet on either side of the opening.

When the wall reaches to the top of a window or door frame fill the gap between the top of the frame and the form with a 2 × 4. Next, place a 2-inch layer of concrete and insert the rebar. Then follows the facestones and the rest of the concrete. Usually smaller stones are placed above the windows and doors due to the smaller space available. (Figs. 3-16 and 3-17).

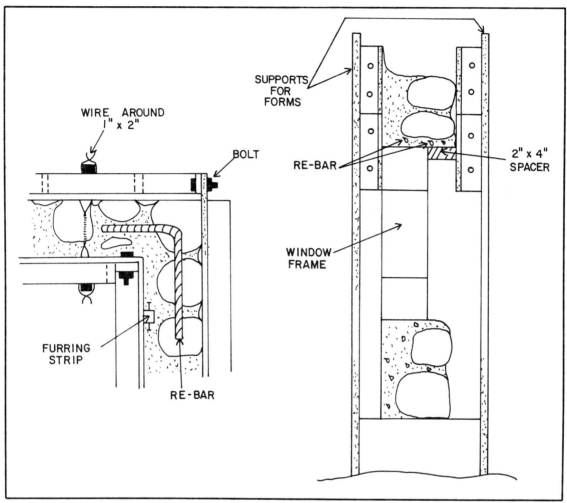

Fig. 3-16. Rebar used to strengthen a wall corner. It should extend at least 3 feet around each side of the corner. Use a 2 × 4 spacer between the form and the frame to place stones above window. Rebar is placed above the window frame, then stones and concrete added. Note lumber used to support the forms.

STAGING

To accommodate building at higher levels, staging had to be erected. This was built with 2 × 4 lumber and 2 × 8 plank. Don't skimp on your staging. It must support your weight plus stones and the concrete being passed up. Our staging was nailed to the forms using 2 × 4 uprights and 2 × 8 planks as walkway. This walkway was supported every 4 to 6 feet. As the forms are raised higher, you can give extra support by nailing 1 × 3 lumber between the forms and the ground. They are then supported by these vertical struts and held quite solidly in place by the wires that pass through the concrete (Fig. 3-18).

Thus we proceeded until all our walls approached the desired height, and we prepared to finish off. If you have kept your formwork level all the way through, you will have little difficulty ensuring that the walls are equal in height all around their perimeter.

FINISHING OFF

Measure up from the footing for a primary check. If

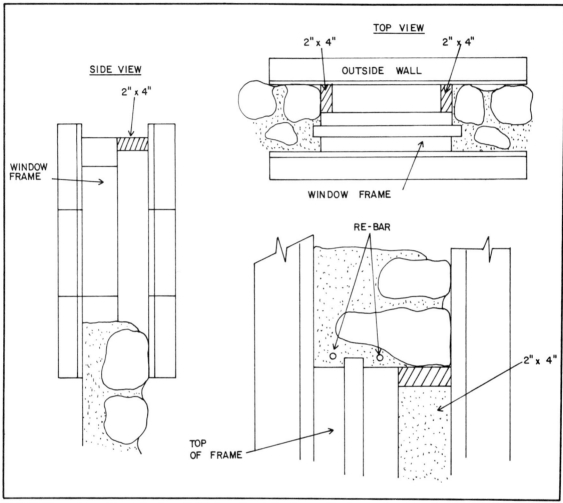

SIDE VIEW

2" x 4"

WINDOW FRAME

TOP VIEW

2" x 4"   2" x 4"

OUTSIDE WALL

WINDOW FRAME

RE-BAR

2" x 4"

TOP OF FRAME

Fig.3-17. Three views of the method used to fill above the window frame with stone and concrete. Note the 2 × 4 used to bridge the gap between the frame and the form.

you have chosen 9 feet as the wall height, nails are driven into the inside wall forms at this height all around the perimeter and connected with lines from wall to wall. Run the lines lengthwise, widthwise, and diagonally. These lines are checked with a level and adjusted by raising or lowering the nails as necessary until you have a series of nails all around the perimeter of the house that are level with each other and at the correct height. The inside of the forms can then be marked with a chalkline connected to the series of nails. The resulting line is the correct height to fill the forms with the stone and concrete (Fig. 3-19).

Next we had to install some small wooden forms to create notches at specific locations, in the same manner as the notches in the footing for the main beam (Fig. 3-20). These notches were to receive the ends of long tie beams that spanned the width of the house, a distance of 20 feet. These beams served two purposes. The first was to hold the tops of the walls securely and prevent any chance of the wall cracking when the roof rafters were installed due to the outward forces of the rafters. Second, they were to be used as floor joists

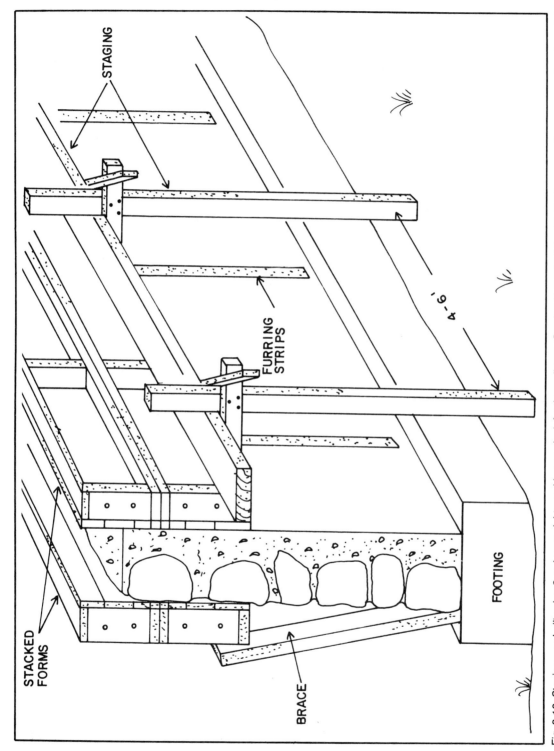

STAGING

FURRING
STRIPS

4'-6"

STACKED
FORMS

BRACE

FOOTING

Fig. 3-18. Staging was built using 2 × 4 as uprights and heavy plank for the walkway. Staging is reached by stepladder; concrete was passed up in metal buckets. It is possible to build elaborate staging to wheel a wheelbarrow up the a landing for the time involved in building it, we found it simpler to use buckets.

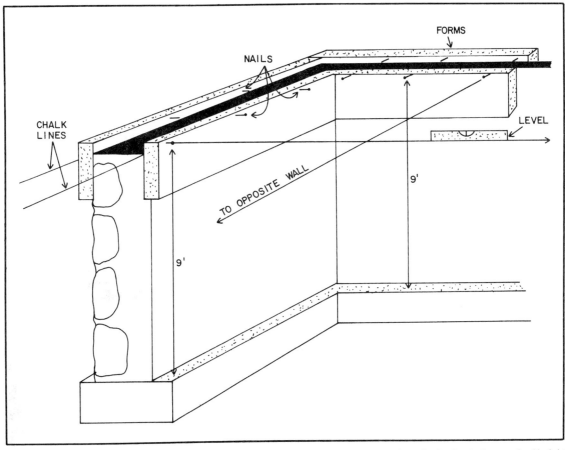

Fig. 3-19. Finishing the wall top with nails, string, and level. A measurement is taken up from the footing to the required height and a nail driven into the form. A string is attached to it and stretched across to the opposite form and leveled and marked with another nail. Continue all around the perimeter of the walls until the correct height is marked on the outside of the forms. By driving the nails through the forms, the height is transferred to the space inside the forms. The concrete is built to this level and wall tops are level.

for a small loft in our open ceilinged house (Fig. 3-21).

We installed two of these 6 × 6-inch beams, each 20 feet long, dividing our walls into thirds lengthwise. We installed a small wood form to create the notch in the wall top and added a large bolt that was anchored in the concrete notch. When placing the beams, we drilled holes in each of the ends to accommodate the bolts and thus fastened the beams securely in place. We used one beam as a floor joist and left the other as part of our open ceiling. To prevent them from sagging in the middle, one was supported from below, another from

the top. (Another way to ensure that your walls are strong is to install rebar vertically as well as horizontally while you are constructing them. This forms a grid or crosshatch pattern in the walls and is the method used to reinforce concrete in commercial building structures. The rebar should be installed about 6 feet apart vertically and 3 to 4 inches from the outside wall face.

Our window frames were placed with stone above the top of them. This necessitated the use of rebar above them for strength. An alternate method of installing frames is to extend them directly to the top of the wall. By doing this, you can avoid building

Fig. 3-20. Forms for stonework for the gable end.

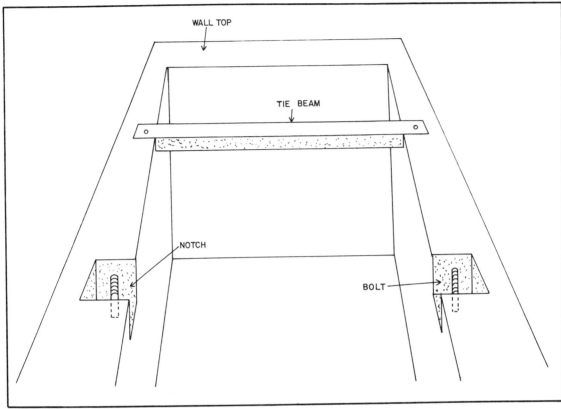

WALL TOP

TIE BEAM

NOTCH

BOLT

Fig. 3-21. Tie beams were installed at the tops of the walls that spanned the total width of the house to hold the walls firmly in place while the roof was built. They later formed the joists for a loft. The notches for the beams contained a bolt fastened in the hard concrete to anchor the beams in place.

stonework above the frames. The plate will sit directly on top of the frame (Fig. 3-22).

The top of the wall is finished with a 2-inch layer of concrete and smoothed level with a trowel. Do your best to achieve level wall tops because the roof, in order not to be warped or uneven, depends on it.

After the forms were filled and while the concrete was still wet, we installed 6-inch bolts, embedded 4 inches into the wall top. They were spaced about 4 feet apart, and when the wall hardened we had a smooth level surface all round interspersed with bolts projecting up 2 inches every 4 feet. Next a 2 × 8-inch plank was drilled with ⅝-inch holes at intervals to match the projecting bolts. It was laid atop the wall and fastened with nuts and washers. We then had a 2 × 8 plate an-

chored firmly to the wall top, ready to receive the rafters (Fig. 3-23).

The plates were installed on the two longer walls only. The shorter walls had to have additional stone and concrete added to them to form the gable ends of the house. Before this was done, however, it was necessary to erect the end rafters. This is described in the following chapter.

POINTING

After the forms are removed, you will have a wall with smooth concrete on one side and a stone face on the other. The stones will have gaps between them and sometimes holes where the concrete was not completely packed around them. These holes are inevitable due to the nature of form work and the impossibility of filling every nook and cranny with concrete. Therefore, to complete the stone facing, the cracks and holes are filled with a smooth mortar mix, using special trowels. This is termed *pointing*. Stone work in other buildings, such as churches and universities, is always completed by pointing. Besides filling in the cracks, pointing serves to protect the stonework from penetration by rain, snow, and frost that would erode and crack the walls. It also gives the wall additional solidity and enhances the appearance of each individual stone.

Pointing is easy and satisfying work. For our mortar we mixed, by hand, three shovelfuls of clean, screened sand with 1 shovelful of cement, and enough water to make a thick paste. Mortar, like concrete, should not be too wet or it runs, nor

too dry as it will not adhere. Again, experience will give you the feel for the correct consistency. Hydrated lime can also be added to the mortar (three sand, one cement, one lime) if you wish, for a stickier mix and to whiten the mortar when dry. Keep the wet mortar in buckets as you use it, moistening it now and then because it tends to dry quickly. Try to use the same type of cement to mix all the mortar because different cement will produce a different color mortar when dry.

To apply mortar, we used modified trowels and a mortar board that we made. A piece of 8 × 12-inch plywood with a wooden handle attached was used to hold the wet mortar. The trowels were made to fit in the narrow cracks by cutting them

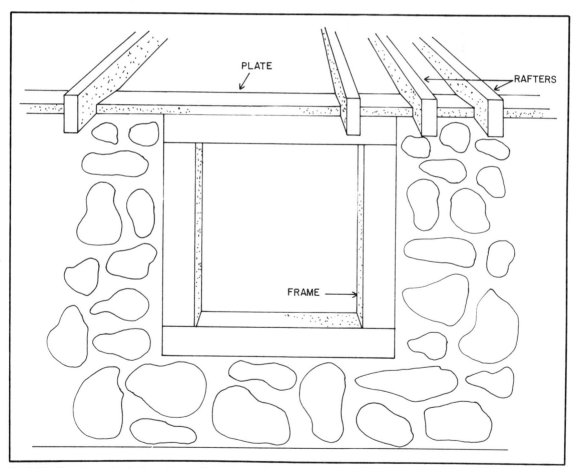

Fig. 3-22. Alternate method of installing a window frame. The frame reaches to the wall top and is part of the plate to which the rafters are attached. There is no stonework above the frame, which makes it an easier method of installation.

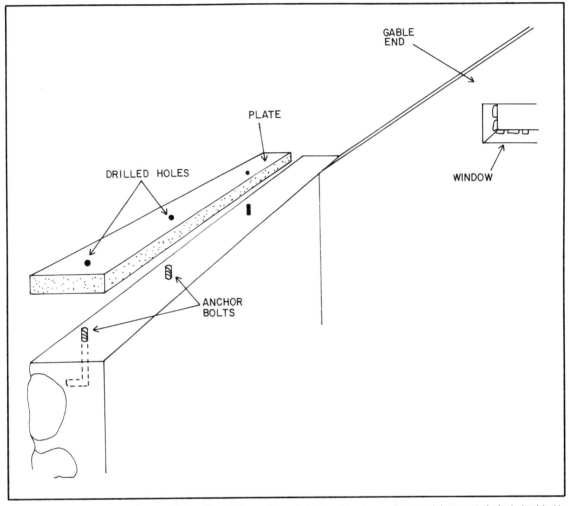

Fig. 3-23. The wall plate, used to attach the rafters to the wall top, is fastened in place using special concrete bolts imbedded in the hardened concrete. The plate is a 2 × 8 or 2 × 10 plank with holes drilled to accommodate the bolts. The plates are only placed on the longer walls because the rafters are fastened directly to the concrete on gable ends.

down from larger trowels with metal shears. We cut three inexpensive trowels into smaller sizes and used them for all the pointing (Fig. 3-24).

To point, first wet the stone wall with a hose or with water from an applicator such as used for spraying plants. This gives a better bond between the mortar and stone. Hold the mortar board under the spot to be filled and push the mortar in and around the stones with your trowel. Depending on your style, the finished surface will be smooth, rough, or perhaps stippled. We let some friends try

pointing and their areas are different from ours. Begin the pointing in a less obvious area of your house. You will gain experience before you do the pointing in the more visible areas such as surrounding the doors and windows.

Pointing may seem a slow, laborious process, but with patience and practice it becomes much quicker. It is also the only time you will have to do any work to the stone face. Once it is done, you will have permanent, maintenance-free, durable, and beautiful walls.

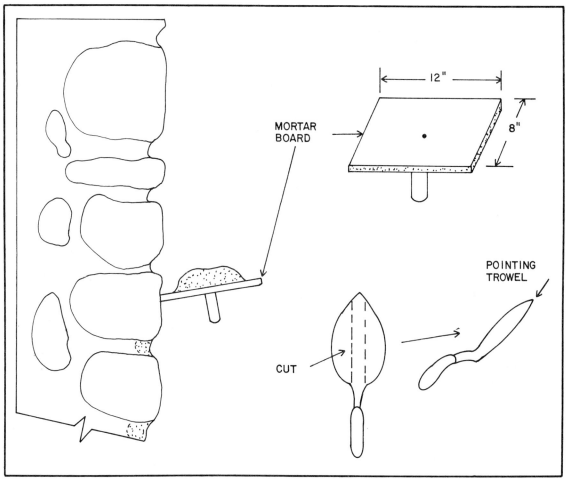

Fig. 3-24. Pointing finishes the surface of the outside wall by filling the cracks between the stones with a fine mortar. This is applied with pointing trowels and a mortar board. Pointing protects the exterior walls from absorbing water and strengthens the stones in place.

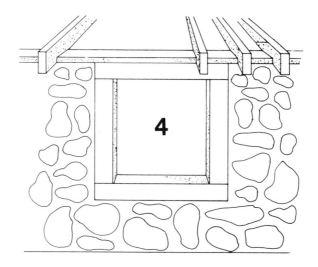

Roof

THERE ARE SEVERAL METHODS OF BUILDING A roof. For our house we built a *gable* roof, the familiar roof with two sloping sides meeting at a center peak. Three other standard roofs are the *shed roof*, the *hip roof*, and the *gable and valley*. A shed roof is a single sloping roof and is described in Chapter 9. A hip roof has four sides that meet at a central peak, somewhat like a low pyramid. A gable and valley roof is a combination of two gable roofs that are attached to each other usually perpendicularly. Each type can be built on a rectangular or square house except the gable and valley, which usually adorns an L- or T-shaped house. Basically, a roof consists of *rafters, collar ties, ceiling joists,* and the exterior covering.

The *rafters* are the sloped beams or planks that form the skeletal structure of the roof. They form a triangle shape joined at the top and resting on the walls at the bottom (Fig. 4-1). To prevent the rafters from spreading apart and also to prevent any inward sag of the roof, *collar ties* are fastened between the rafters. There are many variations for placing collar ties, such as shown in Fig. 4-2.

If an inside ceiling is desired for the house, there must be a means of fastening it overhead. This is done by using *ceiling joists* (Fig. 4-1). The joists are used here simultaneously as collar ties. If the span is a long one between walls, the ceiling joists will need support. This is given by a supporting beam, which is also the framework for the interior partitions.

A method finding considerable favor in contemporary construction is a combination of the rafters, collar ties, and ceiling joists all in one. This result is called a *roof truss* (Fig. 4-3). Because of its design, a roof truss can be pre-built on the ground and later installed intact on the wall plates. This is advantageous because a builder can order his trusses pre-built in a factory, to be delivered and installed when the walls are up.

Other advantages are that the truss is very stable and can be built using lighter materials than would normally be required in a rafter. Two-by-four is sometimes used, and the joints in the truss are secured with pieces of plywood called *gussets*. Also, for an average span, they need no mid-support and

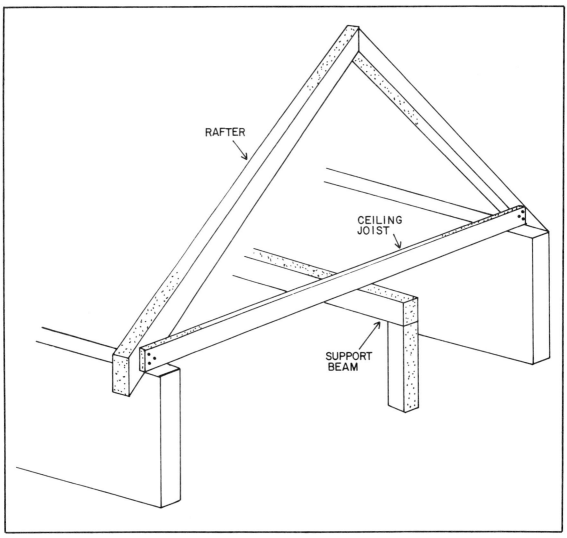

Fig. 4-1. Rafters are wooden planks or beams attached to the wall tops. They slope upward to meet at the peak of the house. They are held together at the bottom using a collar tie. In this instance, the collar tie is also a ceiling joist. The joist is supported in the center by a supporting beam that serves as a framework for an interior partition.

the rooms can be left open wall to wall.

The disadvantage of trusses is that they make an interior ceiling mandatory. Since we wanted a pitched roof, open to view on the inside, roof trusses were not feasible. We wanted to be able to see the heavy rafter beams that give a feeling of space to our house and, at the same time, avoid conventional ceilings of tile or gypsum board that would not blend with our interior design.

We had 3 × 5-inch beams sawn from our logs at the mill and we used these for rafters. (2 × 8-inch plank would also suffice and was used extensively in many older houses. The 2 × 8 rafter is rapidly being replaced by the roof truss in many contemporary houses.)

The slope of the roof is called its *pitch* and is determined in the following manner. Starting from the wall, the rafter slopes upward until it meets its

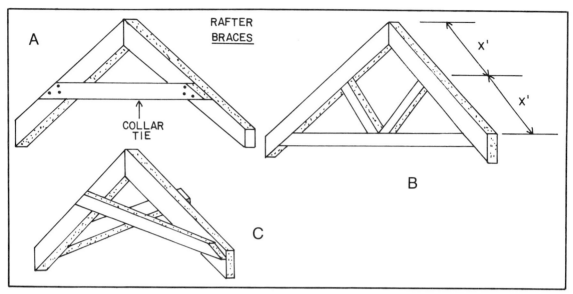

Fig. 4-2. Collar ties serve as bracing for rafters and prevent any inward sag of the roof along with holding the rafters from spreading apart.

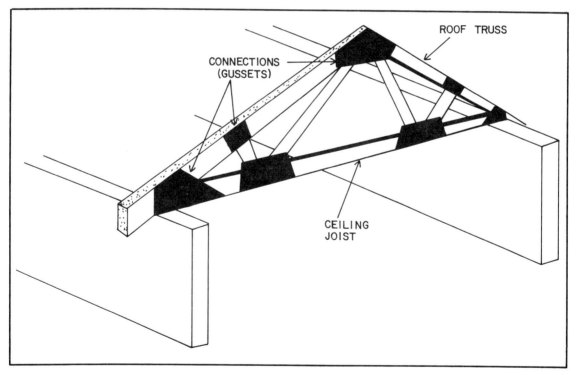

Fig. 4-3. A roof truss is very popular with contemporary builders. It is light, strong, easily built, and installed. They are generally prebuilt and then erected on the walls. For the average span, they don't require support and thus are conducive to open interiors. The only disadvantage is that they make a ceiling mandatory. If you want an open cathedral-type roof, they are not practical.

adjoining rafter at the peak. The vertical rise is expressed in relation to the horizontal span of the rafter. Our pitch was 1-in-2, which means the rafter rises vertically 1 foot for every 2 feet horizontally. The vertical height from footing to peak is 14 feet, giving a height of 5 feet above the top of the walls.

The pitch of your roof can best be determined by drawing it to scale on graph paper. You then see the appearance of the roof line and can calculate the required rafter length.

The pitch will depend upon your design preferences but too shallow a pitch is not desirable if you live where there is considerable snowfall. The snow will build up on the roof and sometimes change to ice. This is a lot of added weight for the roof to bear, and it can cause the roof to leak. If you are not in a snow area, then the pitch will depend solely upon your sense of aesthetics in design.

We cut our rafters 13 feet long to give a generous overhanging eave of about 1½ feet. Wide eaves are attractive on a stone building and also functional. Water and snow are directed away from the walls and footing, lessening the chances of frost buildup and subsequent damage. The eaves also project over the gable ends of the house for the same reasons.

Another factor determining the size of the overhang is the orientation of the house with the sun. Overhanging eaves will let in the sunlight during the winter when the sun is low in the sky. In the summer, when the sun is higher and hotter, the eaves will protect the interior of the house from its rays.

After covering the rafters or trusses with boards, a heavy tarred roofing paper is laid down prior to the final covering. This paper protects the boards from any moisture and seals out any drafts.

The exterior covering is put on next. You can choose from asphalt shingles, wood shingles, cedar shakes, or metal roofing. Since we burn wood for our heating and cooking, we wanted a covering that was fireproof as well as durable so we chose galvanized steel. (Aluminum roofing is also available but is not easily painted (paint flakes off and, if exposed to a lot of wind, the resulting vibration

eventually tears holes around the nail heads). Galvanized steel can be painted after a years' weathering, or it can be purchased already painted, in a choice of colors. Galvanized roofing goes on easily and is available in many lengths. It can also be cut if you require a non-standard size.

ROOF INSULATION

Energy conservation today takes many forms. From driving your car less, clicking off light switches, lowering the thermostat, to aligning your new house with the sun, buying a wood stove, and installing plenty of insulation. There is a proliferation of new magazines on the market that deal specifically with do-it-yourself articles for the home builder. They describe new forms of building to obtain maximum energy conservation at low cost and many interesting articles related to this subject. There weren't as many available when we were designing our house but, if they had been, we would have gained many useful ideas. Your local library probably carries many of them.

Insulating the roof of your house, if you live where winter has a cold grip, is a must. In houses built using roof trusses, the insulation is installed immediately above the ceiling. It is placed between the ceiling joists and is either poured loose from bags or laid in strips called *batts*. The insulation is rated for heat retention (its resistance to heat transfer) and is termed its R-factor. Insulation rated R-20 has a greater resistance to heat transfer than R-10 for example. It is usually much thicker.

The materials used as insulating mediums include spun glass, styrofoam, liquid foams that gel in the walls, and a host of other materials. At one time, the early settlers used birch bark under the shingles and sawdust, moss, and seaweed as insulation in the walls.

Insulation comes in many forms: rolls and squares of spun fiberglass, solid 4 × 8-foot styrofoam sheets, bags of foam beads, as a liquid in a truck, and so on. The choice is up to you and depends upon your design. Each type has its own R-factor and this has to be considered also. Finally, I would recommend that you spend time inves-

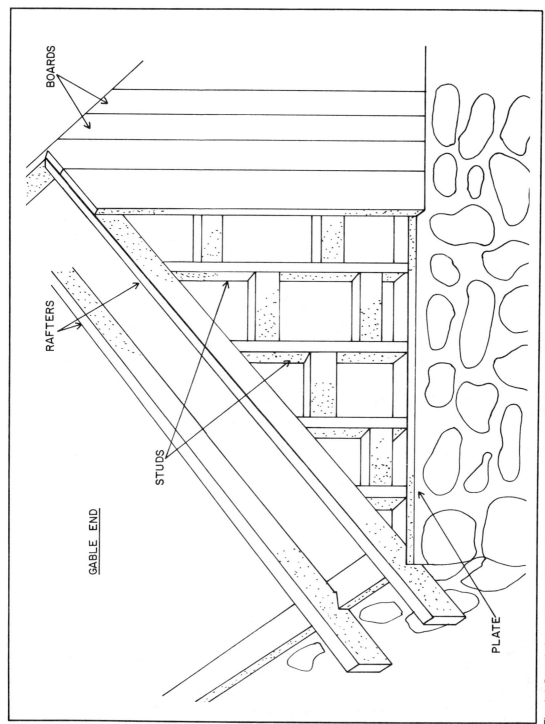

Fig. 4-4. Completing gable ends. The triangular section at the ends may be studded up with 2 × 4 and then covered with boards. Other coverings include shingles and siding. This method is quick and easy when compared with stonework, but since the gable end is the front of our house, we chose stone.

BOARDS

RAFTERS

STUDS

GABLE END

PLATE

tigating the merits and drawbacks of each type.

Recently, it has been shown that certain types of semiliquid foam that are piped between the walls of houses have become a very bad health hazard. The fumes given off from this foam last for years and can severely affect your health. Don't rely on dealer information alone regarding insulation. Ask carpenters, other home owners, and the department of consumer affairs. Be certain of whatever materials you use in your home when it regards potential health risks.

It is for this reason that we chose to avoid many contemporary building products and those natural ones whenever possible. Even some types of wall paneling emit hazardous fumes, as do some wood preservatives and stains. You and your children will be living in your house for many years and it is wise

to investigate the potential dangers beforehand. It is very often up to the individual to protect himself from shoddy merchandising and hazardous materials. Try to be aware, as far as possible, of the qualities of the materials that will go into your house and thus form your indoor environment.

CONSTRUCTION

At this point we had each of our four walls built to a height of 9 feet from the footing. Before we could build the roof, we had to construct the gable ends of the house. This involved erecting the end sets of rafters to act as guides to the roof lines and to outline the gable end. (An alternate method of finishing the triangular shaped piece at each end of the house is to stud it vertically with 2 × 4 and then board it in. It could be boarded vertically, called

Fig. 4-5. Erecting the rafters.

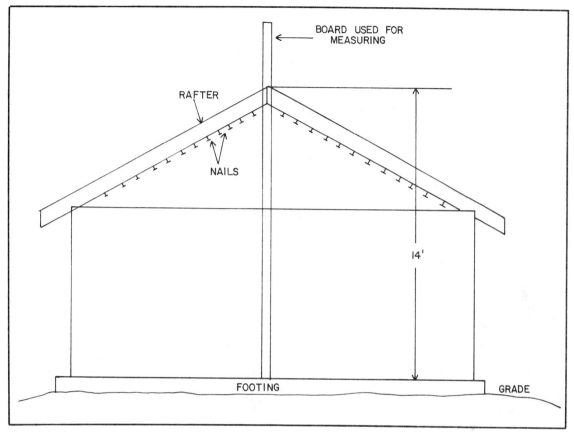

Fig. 4-6. To determine the roof outlines and dimensions, a long board is installed from the footing to the peak of the house and measured to the correct height. A rafter template is built and attached to this board. When satisfied that all the measurements are correct, use the template to cut actual rafters. Note the nails used to anchor the rafter to the concrete of the gable end.

board and batten, or shingled, etc. (Fig. 4-4). Since the gable end was to be the front of our house, we decided that building the stonework to the peak would give the best appearance (Fig. 4-5).

To begin, we erected a piece of wood vertically at the mid-point of the house and measured 14 feet from the footing (Fig. 4-6). Then we fastened lines from the peak to the side walls and tried to visualize the completed roof (Fig. 4-7). We were satisfied with the roof lines, so we cut a piece of 1 × 5-inch lumber as a *template* for the rafters (Fig. 4-8). We measured several times before we cut the notch that fits on the plate into the rafter. It is best to cut two boards as templates. They can then be erected and checked for fit before the actual rafters are cut, thus avoiding miscutting your lumber.

Using the template, we then cut two 3 × 5-inch rafters and drove spikes all along their undersides, leaving 3 inches of spike protruding. (These spikes will later project into the concrete and anchor the rafters firmly.) These two end rafters were erected and braced in position. Then they were spiked at the plates and where they joined to form the peak.

Forms were erected upon the previous ones, which had been left in place at the wall top, and fastened in place. They were filled with stone and concrete and then raised again and so on, until the gable was complete. (We also added a small window in the gable using 2 × 6 for framing.) We now had a gable end with a set of rafters firmly attached to the top of it.

A 1 × 6-inch board was installed as the *ridge*

Fig. 4-7. Rafters going up. Note ridge board at peak.

board and braced horizontally between the two peaks. A ridge board is used to fasten the tops of the paired rafters together. It prevents the rafters from shifting sideways and holds them solid until the roofing boards are nailed on. The rest of the rafters were cut (remembering to allow ½-inch off the top end of each rafter to compensate for the space taken up by the 1-inch thick ridge board) and nailed in place, leaving a 2-foot spacing between each rafter.

The roof was then boarded in with 1 × 6 lumber. The boards were projected 1½ feet beyond the gable ends and a *floating rafter* was attached. (A floating rafter is one which is not anchored at its base to the plate of the house. It is fastened to the eaves of the house after the roof boards are nailed on. It gives a solid, finished appearance to the roof while at the same time keeping the ends of the boards even Fig. 4-9).

Once boarded in, the roof can be finished according to your plans. Our method was to cover the boards with an overlapping layer of tarred roofing paper. This was then *strapped* with 2 × 4's prior to putting on the galvanized steel. The strapping was used to prevent any nails, which fastened the steel, from penetrating the roofing boards and appearing on the inside of our open roof. The 2 × 4's were placed parallel to the ridge board and nailed to the rafters (Fig. 4-10).

Gaps were left in the strapping along the pitch of the gable end. These gaps form the entrance of vents, which allow air to flow above the insulation, along the long axis of the roof. Air flow is necessary because insulation causes condensation to form between it and the metal roof. The condensation must be able to escape, otherwise, it will build up and leak through the roof on the inside and eventu-

78

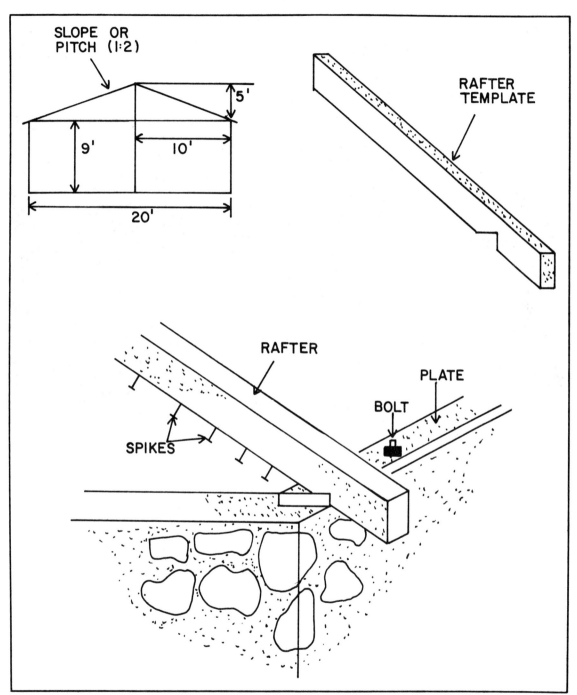

Fig. 4-8. The pitch of a roof is a measurement of its slope and is expressed in a ratio. One-to-two means that the roof rises vertically 1 foot for every 2 feet it spans horizontally. The rafters for the gable ends are attached to the plate on their lower ends and filled in underneath with stone and concrete. A template is used to cut each rafter. This eliminates accumulated errors if each rafter is cut from the previous one, which should never be done.

79

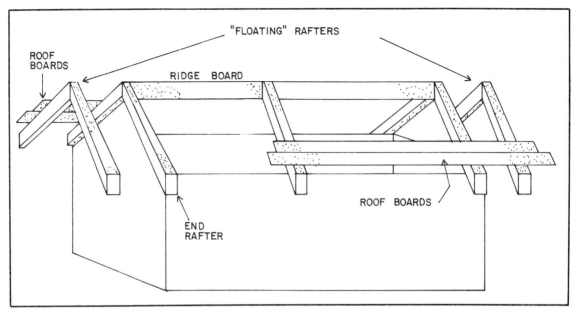

Fig. 4-9. A ridge board is used for fastening the rafters together at their tops. Usually a piece of 1 × 6 or 1 × 8, it holds the rafters in place before the roof is boarded in. A floating rafter is attached to the ends of the roof boards. It is not attached to the plate. It keeps the ends of the boards even, gives strength, and a finished appearance to the eaves.

ally cause rot in the roof boards. Wherever insulation is used, adequate ventilation is a must to prevent rot and the very rapid deterioration of your house.

The insulation we used for the roof was 1-inch solid, 4 × 8-foot styrofoam sheets. We cut it to fit between the strapping and then put on the gal-

vanized steel (Fig. 4-11). The ribs in the steel, plus the gaps along the edge of the pitch, provide enough ventilation to remove condensation.

To complete the roof, the spaces between the rafters, at the plate, were covered with 1 × 6-inch boards cut to fit. We thus eliminated *plancier* and *fascia* boards (those that box in the rafter ends on a

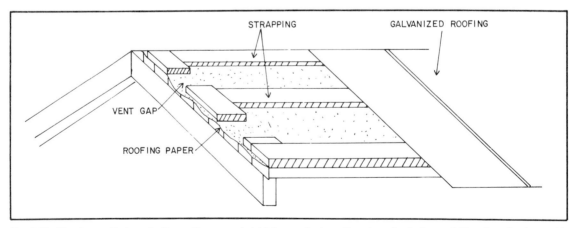

Fig. 4-10. After the roof is boarded in, roofing paper is laid down prior to nailing strapping to the roof. The strapping is used to nail the galvanized roofing on and to provide space for the rigid insulation. Note the gaps in the eave strapping. These provide the openings for the ventilation of the roof insulation.

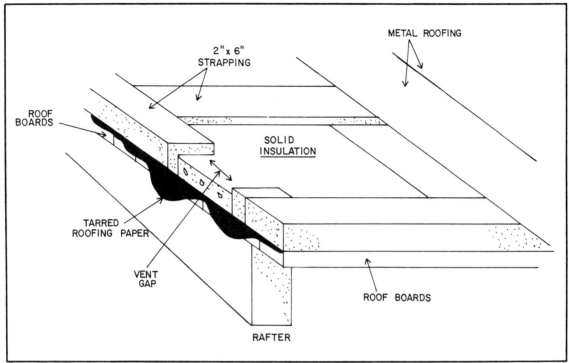

Fig. 4-11. The installation of the rigid foam insulation between the strapping.

conventional house). The steel roofing was allowed to project about 1½ inches beyond the rafter ends to allow water to flow past them (Fig. 4-12).

To complete the rafters on the gable ends, a 1 × 6 board was cut to cover the join between the roof boards and the floating rafters. The roof was now fireproof, insulated, and durable. To reach this stage from the footing to the roof, took us three months.

TRUSSES

If you choose to use roof trusses for your roof, they are installed differently than conventional rafters. As mentioned before, these trusses can be bought already assembled or you can make your own. Once you have the number of trusses you need, you begin by hanging a truss upside down between the two walls. (First lift one end, then the other.) The truss is then rotated until it is in its vertical position and braced in place. It is not nailed solidly until each of the other trusses are positioned because it will probably be necessary to move them one way or another to align them. When all the trusses are up,

bracing boards are used to prevent them from slanting toward the ends of the house and also to keep the ceiling joists equally spaced. When you are satisfied that all the trusses are even with one another and vertically plumb, then they are nailed to the plate and boarded with your roofing material. We used 1-inch lumber for our roof but many builders use 4 × 8-foot sheets of plywood or sometimes a type of pressed wood sheathing. Lumber or plywood are the best choices for strength.

If you choose trusses you will next have to complete the gable ends. The traditional method is to cover the end truss with shingles, siding, or vertical lumber, but I see no reason why it couldn't be done using a combination of conventional rafters and trusses if you wished to have stonework to the peak of your house. First, install end rafters on your gable ends, as previously described, and complete the stonework. Then build trusses to match the pitch of the end rafters and install them. Board the roof in and finish it as you wish.

With roof trusses, a ceiling must be built. Once

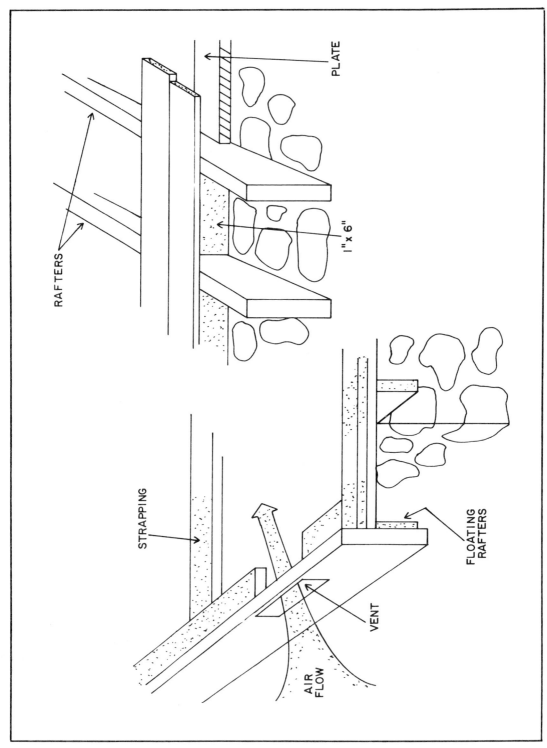

RAFTERS

PLATE

1" x 6"

STRAPPING

AIR FLOW

VENT

FLOATING RAFTERS

Fig. 4-12. The eaves are faced with a 1 × 6 fascia board through which the vents pass. The spaces between the rafters from the plate to the roof boards are covered with pieces of 1 × 6 lumber cut to fit. The edges of these pieces are beveled to match the slope of the roof.

again, you have several options. Ceiling tiles are the standard answer but lumber can be used or gypsum board. If your decor is primarily of wood, then a wood ceiling is easily made. The boards are nailed to the joists and that's it. For ceiling tile the joists must be strapped with pieces of 1 × 3-inch lumber spaced on 12-inch centers or whatever size the tiles will be. The tiles are installed by stapling them in place with a heavy staple gun. (Specific directions are included with the tiles.) Installing gypsum board is a more involved procedure. It is sold under many names, such as Gyproc and Sheetrock. It is a heavy 4 × 8-foot sheet, made with stiff paper on both sides of a gypsum filler. It is easily cut with a mat or tile knife and nailed to the strapping using special ribbed nails. It comes in different thicknesses, and ½-inch is a standard ceiling size. Once in place, it must be crack filled and painted. Crack filling takes a knack and there are tradesmen who specialize solely in crack filling. Their job is to fill the cracks or spaces between the sheets of gypsum board so that they are smooth and unnoticeable when painted. Nail heads must be treated in the same manner. The process begins by mixing a powder with water and applying it to the cracks and nail heads, where it quickly hardens. When dry, it is sanded to a smooth finish.

Sounds easy, but I've done a little crack filling and it's difficult to achieve the professional look. The nail heads were still dimly visible, the cracks were too, plus the dust from the sanding had filtered into every nook and cranny of the room. When properly done, however, the results are smooth walls and ceilings that take paint very well and also lend themselves to the application of wallpaper, which comes in a multitude of new styles, shades, and panoramas. (Gypsum board also serves as an excellent canvas for anyone of an artistic nature and I've seen beautiful murals painted on interior walls.) If crack filling is tricky on walls, working overhead is even more so, and painting ceilings has never been my idea of how to spend an enjoyable day.

When the ceiling is completed, it is insulated from above with loose fiberglass, batts, or styrofoam. To ventilate this area above the ceiling, metal or wooden vents are installed near the peak of the roof in the gable ends and along the underside of the board that encloses the ends of the rafters on the outside of the house. The area of the vent should equal at least 4 square feet for every 1000 square feet of attic floor area. The air then enters at the plate of the house, rises up, and exits at the two peaks, removing any water vapor that may be in the attic. (With the great concern over energy conservation, all you have to do to receive detailed information concerning insulation is to write your local government office. There is a wealth of information to be had from the government on this subject and no doubt you will receive many booklets, pamphlets, and brochures at no cost).

Other options for the external roof covering are asphalt shingles, wood shingles, shakes, and rolled roofing. Generally, wood shingles and shakes are the most expensive, then asphalt and, lastly, rolled roofing. Each has its merits and drawbacks, and each is installed differently.

Almost everyone is familiar with wood shingles. Many of us were reared in a house that had wooden shingles and remember the chore of scraping off old blistered paint, a long tedious process, and then repainting. Nowadays, wood shingles are almost never seen on a roof but wood shakes are becoming popular on many contemporary homes, particularly cedar homes and ranch style houses. Wood shakes had been made for years by our forefathers for use on their log houses, and once again they are receiving considerable notice.

Traditionally, red cedar was considered the best wood for shakes, but spruce, pine, and fir can also be made into shakes. A *shake* is a piece of wood about 15 to 20 inches long, of varying widths. It should be about ½- to ⅝-inch thick. It is made by cutting a round section of a tree into vertical strips with the use of a special tool called a *froe*. The froe is basically a heavy steel blade, about 20 inches long, 3 inches wide, and ¼-inch thick, with a handle attached so that the tool looks like an "L". To chop a piece of firewood you place it on a chopping block vertically and hit it with an ax. To make a shake you do the same, except you rest the froe on the log and hit it with a heavy wooden club. The blade sticks in the log and a twist of the handle splits off a shake. To keep the log from becoming narrow at one end due to the taper of the shake, it is turned upside down for each new shake, or every second one. The shakes are then installed just as wood shingles are or they are first thinned and tapered with a hand-held tool called a *drawknife*. This makes the shakes more evenly matched and puts a lengthwise taper on them. When installed, the thick end is exposed to the weather with the thin end up, as are regular shingles.

Asphalt shingles come in a variety of shapes and sizes, such as diamond patterns and square patterns. The type used most often is the three-tab, rectangular asphalt shingle, usually 12 × 36-inch, in bundles that will cover 100 square feet. These bundles are called a *square* and are sold either in a square (100 square feet), half-square (50 square feet), or third square (33⅓ square feet). They are laid *double thickness,* which means that one shingle overlaps the other by 5 inches. The shingles always start at the edge of the roof and proceed towards the peak. They are nailed with special shingle nails, and, as an added measure, some builders put a dab of asphalt roofing cement under each shingle.

To begin, a heavy roofing paper is laid on the

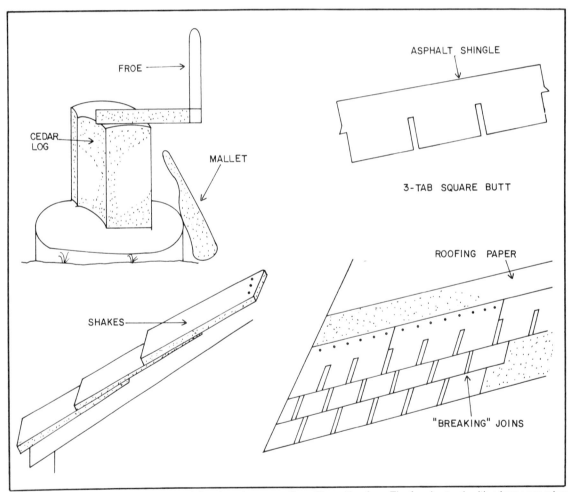

Fig. 4-13. Cedar shakes are made by splitting them from a section of log with a froe. The froe is struck with a heavy wooden mallet and the shake is split off the log. The asphalt shingle is a three tab square butt shingle. When installed on a roof, they are staggered so that each gap in the shingle is covered by a tab of the shingle above it. This is termed *breaking joins*.

84

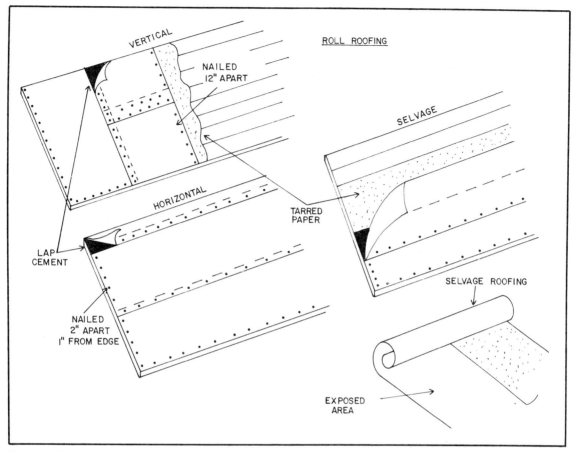

Fig. 4-14. Rolled roofing is inexpensive compared to shingles and metal roofing and is easily installed. It may be laid either vertically or horizontally and is nailed and glued in place. The rolled roofing used on low pitched roofs is called selvage. This type has a large overlap, which is glued to be completely watertight.

roof. Any edges must overlap. Then the shingles are applied. The first row is nailed upside down along the edge of the roof, then the second row goes on top of the first. The second row is moved 6 inches to the left so that the tabs on the shingles *break* or cover the joins on the ones below. The third row is laid as was the second. A chalkline is snapped along the roof every second or third course so that the edges of the shingles remain in a straight line. When the peak is reached from both sides, it is covered with a shingle that folds over the peak and overlaps on both sides. This is *capping* the roof. Asphalt shingles are durable, weather resistant, and fireproof and available in different colors (Fig. 4-13).

Roll roofing is another choice available for finishing the roof and is very simply installed. After covering the roof with heavy felt paper, the asphalt roofing is simply unrolled and nailed in place. It should be applied horizontally. Where the edges overlap, cement is used to bond the roofing together. It is also cemented at the roof edges.

Roll roofing comes in several types and sizes. The standard size is 36 inches wide and 36 feet long. It is also called a square. There are grades of weight or thickness—medium, heavy, and heavy duty—and the surfaces can be smooth or covered with a pebbly mineral surface like asphalt shingles. There is also a type of roll roofing with a wavy edge that simulates a shingled appearance.

The type of roll roofing you buy depends upon the pitch of your roof. For a very low pitch there is a type of roll roofing called *selvage*. This is 36 inches wide with an 18-inch lap joint. This is necessary to prevent the roof from leaking. The pitch must be low in order to use this, about 1 inch to 1 foot. Selvage is both nailed and heavily cemented.

To install roll roofing, the first layer is unrolled along the edge of the roof and nailed in place. The lap joint is cemented and the second layer applied. Continue to the peak from both sides and then a capping layer is put down and fastened. This makes a very quick, inexpensive roof covering (Fig. 4-14), but it is not especially attractive.

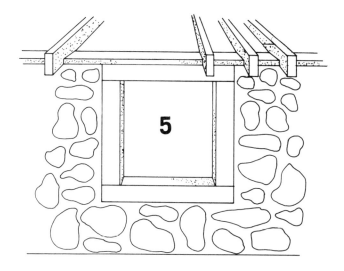

Windows and Doors

AFTER THE WALLS ARE UP AND THE ROOF ON, the windows and doors are installed to seal the house against the weather. You can then do the interior work in comfort, regardless of the weather. By this stage, you will have already decided on the types of windows and doors that you want. In fact, this will be a determining factor in the size of the window frames that are built into the walls.

We chose to build all our windows and doors ourselves, because of the considerable savings. For example, to buy from a supplier, our three large south-facing windows, double glazed, would have cost $1,000. (*Glazing* refers to each pane or sheet of glass in a window frame. Double glazed means two panes of glass.) By building our own, the total cost of our three windows (each 3 × 4-foot) plus three storm windows (six windows total), was $65. We paid $50 for six secondhand sheets of glass, $10 for the lumber, and $5 for the sealing compound.

Second, making our own windows and doors gave us the freedom to design sizes and shapes that were not of standard dimensions, plus we could design to complement the appearance of our stone house.

If you choose to buy your windows, however, there is a wide variety of styles and sizes on the market. Ironically, from our investigations it appears that solid wood windows are much more expensive than the familiar aluminum windows, especially the better known brands. Pre-built windows are available in many sizes but it is also possible to order custom-made windows. You give the dealer the size of your window opening and they will make a window to fit, usually for little additional cost. In this way, you need only determine the size you need, take delivery, and install them. If you are pressed for time, then perhaps this is the best alternative.

To make your own windows you need glass. You can obtain it new or secondhand (with glass, secondhand is as good as new) but there is one difference. If you buy new glass, you can ask for any size that you need and the dealer will supply it. If you buy old windows, then often the glass will not be the size you had in mind. Therefore, it will have to be cut either by yourself or someone else. I recommend someone else, preferably an experienced glass cutter, who will often cut it for you for a modest fee. If you first have to try your hand at glass cutting, as I did, there are a few basic hints that will help.

First of all, cutting glass is like no other procedure that you will encounter while building. It engages your total concentration during the stages preparatory to the actual moment of truth. Then, in one short half-second, your emotions will either experience a gratifying "ah!" (when the glass snaps exactly where you want it to), or you will feel an emotion akin to that felt when your baseball shattered a window.

Keeping this in mind then, here's how it's done. The first time you cut glass, experiment on a piece that is expendable; the second and third times do the same. Glass cuts more readily if it is absolutely clean. If it is old glass, wash it with soap and water, then wipe it clean with a cloth dipped in vinegar, and let it dry. Glass must be cut on a flat surface, such as a piece of plywood covered with newspaper that acts as a cushion between the wood and glass. Use a glass cutter with a single round cutting edge, the multiple-type just complicates matters. After measuring the size you want, use a yardstick or similar straight edge to guide the cutter and make only one stroke to mark the glass. It is important that the mark be continuous, with no gaps, lightly etched into the glass surface and done only once. If you try to make it deeper by repeating the etch, you increase the chances of breakage. To break the glass after etching, align the mark over the edge of the cutting board with the etch on top of the glass. In other words, don't turn the glass over. Grasp the piece to be removed firmly and support the remainder in place with your other hand. A quick downward snap will separate the glass along the etch mark. Do not push slowly downward or disaster results.

There is a definite knack involved in glass cutting that only comes with practice. It is also related to confidence. For example, I destroyed several pieces of glass trying to cut them to window size. Every time I tried, the glass would thwart me and self-destruct. Yet, when I cut up the remaining pieces to place them in the garbage, I made perfect cuts every time.

Glass comes in different thicknesses. Ordinary window glass is usually about 3/32 to 1/8 inch thick. Thinner glass is made (1/16-inch) but is not recommended for windows. Thicker glass (1/8-inch and up) is generally used as the window area becomes larger. Our three large windows are of 1/4-inch glass, termed *plate* glass. Plate glass is much stronger than window glass but also more expensive. Store front windows are plate glass and, if you can locate a store that has a broken or cracked glass, they will often give it away if you will remove it, or charge a small price. Then you get it cut to your required size and have a 1/4-inch plate glass window at a very reasonable price. For most of your windows, 3/32-inch glass is fine and, to solve the problem of a large glass area, windows can be made by incorporating a series of small panes in one large area. Another advantage of this type of window is made apparent if breakage takes place; only one small pane needs replacing.

Obtaining glass can be an interesting hobby. Even before the walls were begun we were scouting the newspapers and bulletin boards for secondhand glass. Besides our large windows, we obtained many other pieces of glass and old windows of various sizes. If you find old windows it is usually best to remove the glass from the frames and build your own. The new frames will last longer. Old frames often have several layers of paint on them and they appear solid but, if you dig the paint away, the wood may be rotting on the inside due to trapped moisture. We are still collecting glass whenever we discover a bargain and plan to use it for a future greenhouse. Glass is also handy to have in case of breakage. Be sure that your glass is safely stored and, if you have to leave it outside, cover it with plastic and a layer of boards.

To make your own windows, it is a definite advantage if you own, or have access to, a bench or table saw. Windows can be made without one but it takes considerable skill and effort to do so. Using a bench saw, we built three large fixed windows (unopenable), three smaller fixed windows, three opening windows, plus storm windows to cover them all. They were all built using the same method and varied only in size.

Whether or not your windows open depends upon your design ideas. Large picture windows are generally fixed in place and smaller ones are built to open. There must be some means of admitting fresh air into a house and opening windows is a traditional method. We chose a combination of movable windows and vents. We tried to locate them so that a cross flow of air could be initiated by opening windows or vents located opposite one another. Since our house is open on the inside, it has worked very well and we can have a large flow of air in the house or reduce it to suit the temperature. Some houses have all the windows fixed, and fresh air is introduced by venting systems. It sounds successful enough, but we prefer to have the old fashioned open window that lets in bird song and the sound of leaves fluttering, along with the fresh air. Be sure to check local fire codes if you opt for fixed windows; most areas require opening windows of a specified size for bedrooms.

CONSTRUCTION

We built all our windows in the following manner, using planed dry 2 × 4's chosen for their straightness and freedom from knots. Green lumber is not suitable for making windows because it will warp and shrink as it dries out.

First, on a table saw, cut a ¾ × ¾-inch notch along one side of each of four pre-measured pieces of 2 × 4. Save the resulting strips of wood. (These pieces were cut long enough to allow for exact measurement later on. If the window was to be 3 × 4-foot, we cut two pieces 4 feet long and two pieces 5 feet long.)

Next, cut 45° angles on the ends of each piece of wood as shown in Fig. 5-1, after measuring them to their exact dimensions. The outside of the window frame is exactly the same size as the inside of the larger frame in the wall.

The frames are assembled using waterproof wood glue and 3½-inch galvanized nails at each corner. The frame then has a ¾ × ¾-inch notch all the way round its inner perimeter. (The glass fits into this notch.)

Next, put a *bead* (layer) of good quality caulking compound all around the surface of the notch against which the glass will lay. This acts as a cushion for the glass to lay on and forms a waterproof seal. Install the glass and fasten it in place with the strips previously saved from the cut-out notch. Use 1½ inch galvanized nails. Firmly push the strips against the glass to even out the caulking and then carefully nail them using a nail set. Apply a coat of varnish or other sealant to weatherproof the frame and the window is ready for installation.

To install fixed windows, ¾-inch strips are cut from a board on a bench saw. These strips are nailed to the 6 × 6-inch window frames about 3 inches from their outside edge and all around their inside perimeter. The assembled window frame is then inset against these strips and fastened there with more pieces of ¾ × ¾-inch lumber. A bead of caulking is applied to seal these strips against the window frame. (Remember to use galvanized nails wherever any nails are exposed to weather (Fig. 5-2).

Movable windows are installed in the same fashion, using strips on the inside as a stop, but they are hinged at the top directly to the 6 × 6 frame. The windows open outward, don't take up any inside space, and will shed any water that falls on them. They are kept open with a special hinge designed for this type of window. A piece of wood will serve the same purpose (Fig. 5-3).

A wooden screen can be made for use in summer. They are portable and fit on the inside of the window frame, resting against the wooden strips. To make a screen, fasten four pieces of 1 × 3 together to form a rectangle the size of the window opening. Lay screening over the rectangle and fasten it in place with thin strips of wood and finish nails. Small handles can be attached to make installing and removing the screen a simple matter.

For the winter, we made storm windows using the same methods. These storm windows, however, go on the *inside* of the house and fit in place like the screens in the summer. They thus create the desired insulating dead air space, with the

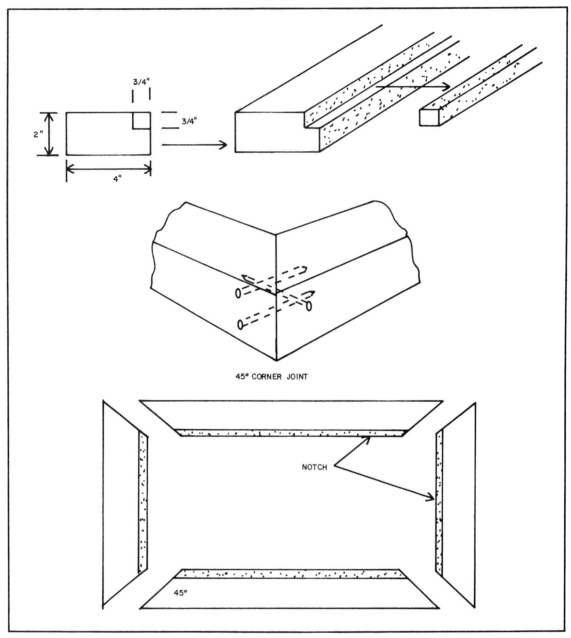

3/4"

3/4"

2"

4"

45° CORNER JOINT

NOTCH

45°

Fig. 5-1. Window frames are made using 2 × 4 lumber with a notch cut from one edge as shown. 45° angles are cut on the ends of the pre-measured pieces and fastened together to form 90° corners, which are nailed and glued in place.

bonus of needing very little upkeep because they are not exposed to the weather. Their removal in spring is a ritual that, for us, ensures the arrival of good weather.

We built one other type of window when we added our porch to the house. The window is 3½ × 3½ feet and split in two, vertically, making two window frames each 21 inches by 3½ feet. They are

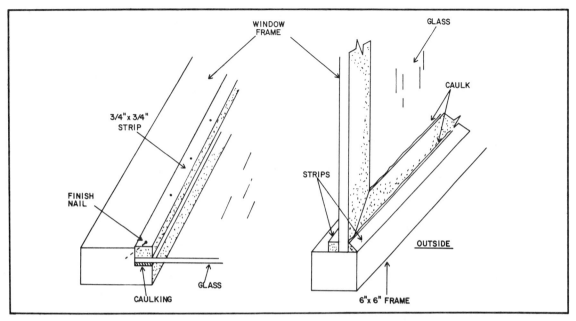

Fig. 5-2. The glass for the window is laid in the notch. It rests on a bed of caulking and is fastened in place using the strip of wood saved from cutting the notch. The finished window is installed in the 6 × 6 window frame using strips of wood as stops. It is then caulked to make it watertight.

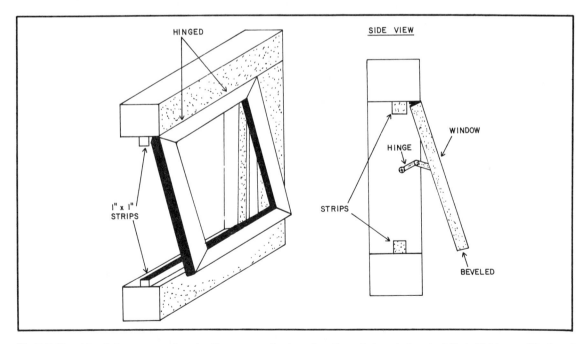

Fig. 5-3. Movable windows are made using the same methods as the other windows but are installed with hinges at the top of the 6 × 6 frame. The window opens outward and is held open with a special hinge. By opening outward, the window sheds water and doesn't take up any space on the inside of the house.

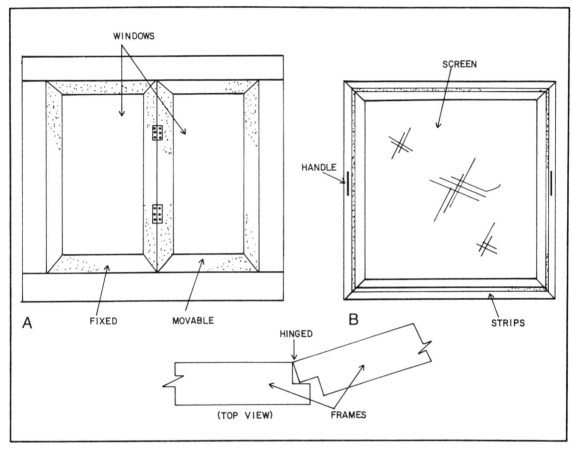

Fig. 5-4. A double window, with one side fixed and one side movable. It is hinged in the center and a top view shows how the edges of the windows lap to prevent a gap between them. A screen can easily be made. Four strips of wood are nailed together to form a frame of the correct size, covered with a piece of screening, and handles attached.

hinged in the center, with one side fixed in place and one side opening. Notches were cut where the two frames meet so that there is an overlap that seals the join between them. They are fastened in place using strips, the same as all the other windows (Fig. 5-4).

I remember reading that for two rectangular windows of the same size, for example 3 × 6 feet, different amounts of light are admitted, depending on their placement either horizontally or vertically. The article stated that long, vertical alignments let in more light intensity than a window that is longer horizontally. I haven't been able to verify this in any practical way but, since we prefer long vertical windows, we are at least going with the odds.

DOORS

We built three doors. An outer storm door, an inner screen door, and a combination summer/winter door. The possibilities inherent in door-making are limited only by your imagination and, of course, your funds. Since building our doors, we have seen many fine examples of workmanship done by other home owners. Door-making for some approaches an art form. It announces the entrance to your home most impressively. Our door design was once again influenced by the criteria of low cost and simplicity.

For door-making we used 1-inch dry pine boards. Since doors must be weatherproof, the edges of the boards, when joined together, cannot have any cracks between them. To facilitate this

92

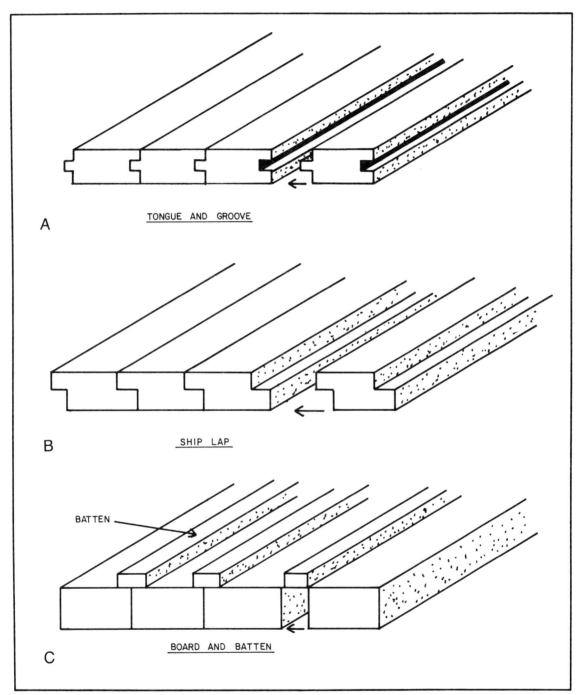

A **TONGUE AND GROOVE**

B **SHIP LAP**

C BATTEN **BOARD AND BATTEN**

Fig. 5-5. Types of edging for lumber are tongue and groove, shiplap, and board and batten. Edging is necessary where joints between two pieces of lumber must not gap. The first two strengthen the joint between the pieces of lumber but require special tools to make. Board and batten is an easy method to use if you don't have a bench saw or don't wish to buy the other more expensive edged lumber.

there are common methods of edging lumber. Three of these are *tongue and groove, shiplap,* and *board and batten.* (Fig. 5-5).

Board and batten is the simplest because it requires no special tools. To create the tongue and groove or shiplap requires the use of a bench saw.

For our outer porch door we used tongue and groove. The pine boards were cut to size, assembled to the proper width, and fastened together using the *Z-brace method* (Fig. 5-6). The completed door was hinged directly to the door frame, and 1 ×

3 strips were nailed around the inner perimeter of the frame to act as a door stop (Fig. 5-4B). A latch was installed and weather stripping fastened to the inner strips to prevent drafts. In warmer weather, this door can be held completely open by a catch on the outside wall.

The inner porch door is a screen door, very easy to make. One-by-six-inch pine boards were cut to the proper dimensions and assembled as shown in Fig. 5-5A. Over the openings, screening was laid and held in place by ½ × 1-inch strips. The screen

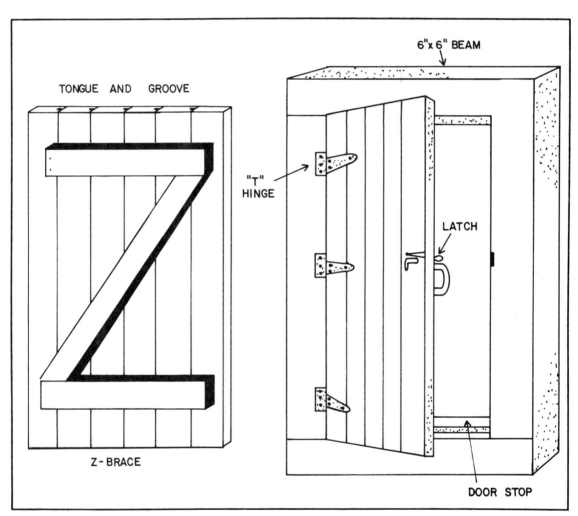

Fig. 5-6. A door made using tongue and groove lumber and a "Z" brace. The Z brace prevents the door from twisting or sagging as well as holding it together. The door is installed by hinging it directly to the 6 × 6 door frame. Pieces of 1 × 3 lumber are used for door stops and a latch holds the door shut.

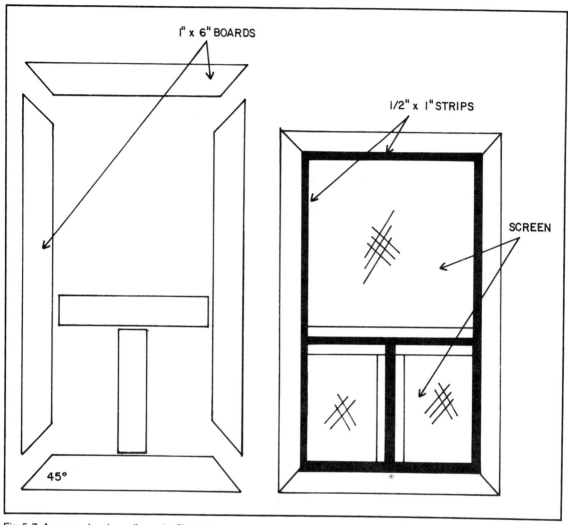

Fig. 5-7. A screen door is easily made. Simply fasten 1 × 6 lumber to form a door frame and cover it with screening held in place with ½ × 1-inch strips of wood. This door may be covered with a sheet of paneling in the winter to serve as an inner door. Along with weather stripping, the double doors create a satisfactory seal against drafts.

door was hinged on the inside, directly to the door frame, and opens inward. When the weather turns cold, the screen door is covered on the inside with a sheet of paneling and thus we have, in effect, a set of solid double doors (Fig. 5-7).

The combination door for the main entrance to the house was made as shown in Fig. 5-8. Three pine boards were assembled with the central board hinged on one side. This panel opens outward and is fastened by a catch to become a screen door. The

three boards were all nailed solidly on a 1 × 3 frame except for the hinged center panel. Over this frame, on the inside, screening was fastened to cover the opening made when the panel is open. In winter, with the panel shut, 1-inch solid styrofoam insulation is fastened between the 1 × 3 framing on the inside of the door. The insulation is covered with a sheet of paneling and the door is then protected from drafts by weather stripping and insulated.

It is essential that all drafts, especially around

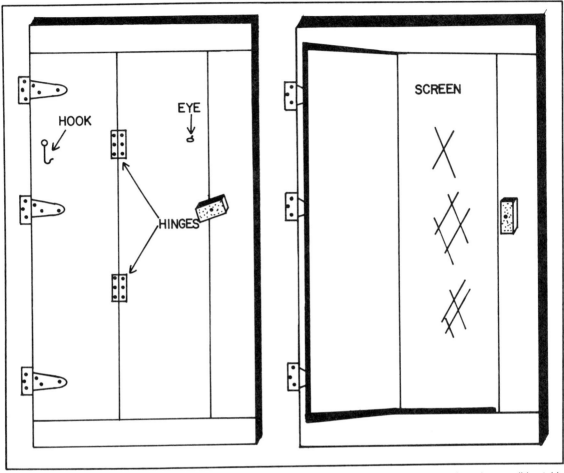

Fig. 5-8. A combination door made of wood. It can be opened to serve as a screen door, or shut, and used as a solid outside door. In the winter, insulation is fastened in place on the inside and covered with a section of paneling.

windows and doors, are reduced to a minimum for the winter. Drafts not only cause a heat loss but they are the main reason why a house feels cold. By using weather stripping, caulking compounds, and snug fits between joints and seams, the majority of drafts will be eliminated.

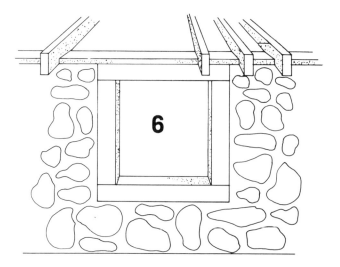

Interior Finishing

FINISHING THE INTERIOR OF YOUR HOUSE WILL require at least as much of your time as it took to erect the exterior shell and possibly more if you are doing it alone. A floor has to be laid; insulation installed; walls covered; partitions, cupboards, and closets built; wiring and plumbing done; and a host of other details methodically integrated into the house, following a step-by-step procedure.

At this stage, your plans must be followed quite exactly since the plumbing and wiring holes in the concrete are already determined and any changes will involve complicated readjustments.

There are hundreds of ideas for interior layout and design, and a plenitude of books and magazines to turn to for inspiration. Since it is impossible to give you a description of them all, I will describe the methods we used, along with helpful hints and shortcuts that save money and space.

FLOOR

First the floor. We began inside the footing, where we laid a sheet of plastic over the earth, completely covering it. This keeps the crawl space dry and

prevents any dampness from rising upward. The plastic was extended up the inside of the footing and held there by the placement of the floor joists (Fig. 6-1).

Next, we built a center support beam of three 2 × 8-inch planks spiked together to form a 6 × 8-inch beam, 26 feet long. This was installed with each end resting in the notches previously made in the footing. It was supported by concrete pads, at approximately 6-foot intervals, that had also been built beforehand. Two-by-eight-inch floor joists were laid from footing to beam and spiked on 16-inch centers. (Each joist was exactly 16 inches apart from its neighbor, measured from center to center (Fig. 6-2).

Where the joists rested on the footing, we installed a 1 × 5-inch ledge plate to which we nailed the joists. The thickness of this plate must be accounted for when calculating the height at which the main beam will be installed. The concrete pads that support the main beam were poured low enough to leave room for adjustment, either up or down, of the main beam. To get the joists level, it was necessary

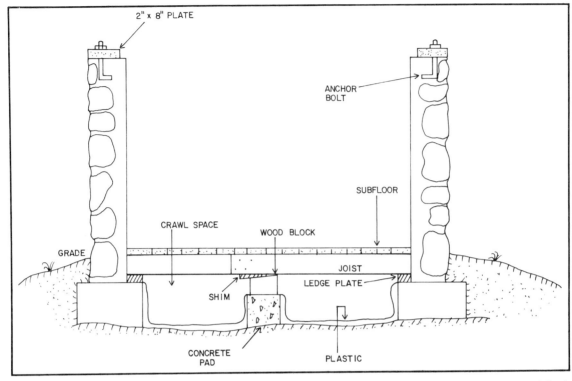

Fig. 6-1. Preparation of the crawl space, prior to installing the floor joists, includes covering the bare earth with a layer of plastic that prevents moisture from entering the crawl space, and placing ledge plates on the edges of the footing. These 1 × 4 ledge plates are used to support the joists and provide an even surface. The joists are supported in the center by wooden blocks and are adjusted to exact position using hardwood wedges as shims where necessary.

to rest the main beam on pieces of 2 × 8 where they sat on the pads and then add oak wedges to obtain the correct height. When we were certain that the floor joists were level in all directions, only then did we nail them solidly in place. (A carpenter friend of ours recommended that the floor should actually be raised between ¼- to ½-inch in the center so that, when settling did occur, it would bring the floor level. We took the advice and raised the main beam ¼ inch above the ledge plates.)

When the joists were in place, the next operation was the installation of *bridging* to secure them against twisting or shifting laterally. Bridging can be accomplished in two ways: using solid pieces of wood, or crossed pieces of 1 × 3 nailed diagonally from the top of one joist to the bottom of another. (See Fig. 6-2.) Bridging imparts extra rigidity to a floor and should be installed wherever a span ex-

ceeds 6 to 10 feet. Our bridging was placed between the joists at 5-foot intervals. After the bridging was done, we boarded in the floor using 1-inch lumber. This lumber should be sized on a planer to obtain uniform thickness and need only be planed on one side, which is less expensive than lumber planed on two or four sides.

The first layer of boards nailed to the joists is called a *subfloor*. The subfloor provides a base on which to lay your finished floor, eliminates drafts, and makes the total floor more solid. Subfloors are sometimes made using plywood specially made for this purpose. It is called plywood underlay and is cheaper than first-class plywood.

Plywood comes in different types and thicknesses. Most plywood is made in 4 × 8-foot sheets, and common sizes are ¼, ⅜, ½, ⅝, ¾ and 1 inch thick. Other common designations are under-

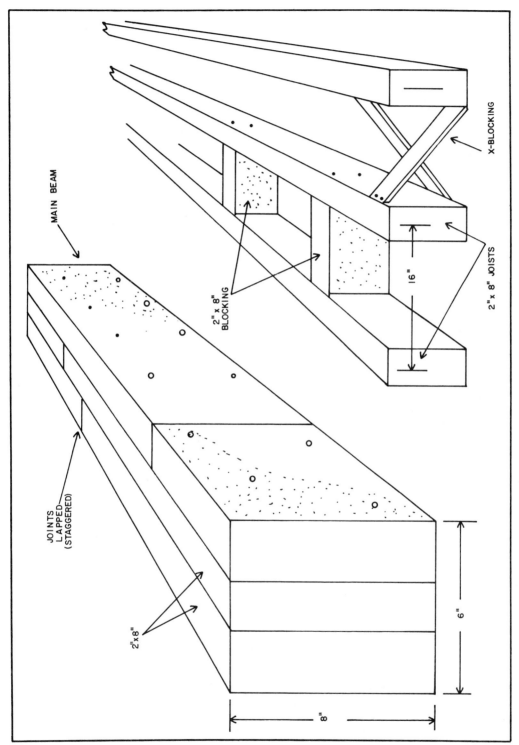

Fig. 6-2. The main beam for our house was 26 feet long. It is getting more and more difficult to find timbers of large dimensions, thus pieces of 2 × 8 lumber are nailed together to form a beam of the required size. Joints should be staggered so that no two joints are together. Blocking, or bridging, are the terms used to describe the method of strengthening floor joists to prevent them from twisting or flexing. Solid pieces of lumber are nailed between the joists or they can be X-braced as illustrated.

lay, good-one-side, and good-two-sides. *Good-one-side* means that one side of the plywood sheet is sanded smooth, contains no holes or rough spots, and is ready for painting. The reverse side is rough, may contain cracks and holes, and is meant to be hidden when used (as when covering over a wall). *Good-two-sides* is a 4 × 8-foot sheet with both sides finished and ready for use in a job such as cabinets, where both sides are visible. *Underlay* has both sides unfinished. Each type has its own price, underlay being the lowest priced and good-two-sides the most expensive. The thickness of the plywood also determines its price and is chosen depending upon its intended use. One-quarter-inch plywood, for example, is too thin for use as a sub-floor but, since it it flexible, it is excellent for

building boats. Generally, the thicker the plywood, the sturdier your floor, but again it depends on use. One-half-inch underlay is suitable for use under a second wood floor but, if only the subfloor is to be laid, as may be the case if tiles or carpeting are planned, then 1-inch plywood is best.

The options available for finishing the floor are many. A subfloor can be the base for a second wood floor, tiles, carpet, or rolled flooring. Double floors are much stronger than a single floor and exhibit much less springiness or bounce. A wooden sub-floor using 1-inch lumber is warmer than plywood and very often cheaper. Another method we encountered was the use of 2-inch lumber, milled as tongue and groove and laid as one floor.

Our choice was to build a double floor using

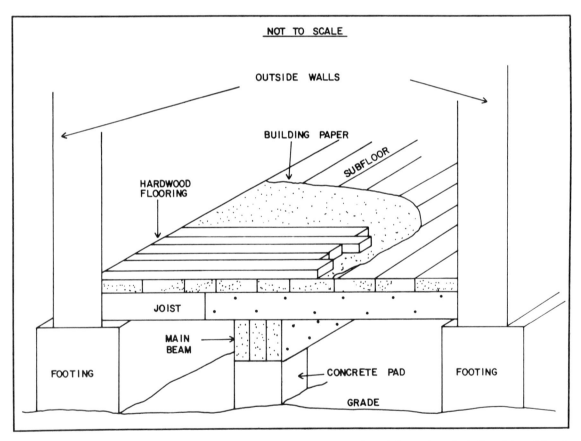

Fig. 6-3. A double floor is generally built for strength and to reduce the springiness inherent in a single floor. The subfloor is made of rough lumber or plywood underlay. Next, a layer of building paper is put down to prevent any draft from the basement or crawl space. The finished floor may be of wood, tile, carpet, rolled flooring, etc.

1-inch boards for the subfloor and maple for the finished flooring. We covered the subfloor with a layer of building paper to prevent any drafts and to provide an insulating factor. Then we laid the ¾-inch tongue and groove maple flooring. The width of the maple boards was 2¼ inches. To obtain it required a week's work for Barbara and me. A neighbor was demolishing an old house and offered us the maple flooring that was in it. The flooring was sound and in good condition and we had only to take it up. We jumped at the opportunity and proceeded to work with wrecking bars. We soon discovered just how solidly those old floors were made. The flooring was nailed approximately every 12 inches with 3-inch nails and it required considerable effort to pry each board loose, being careful not to split it. As we worked, we consoled our tired arms with the thought of a free hardwood floor.

After the flooring was taken up, we spent three days removing the nails that remained in most of the boards. We cleaned the grooves and tongues of the flooring by scraping them with screwdrivers and paint scrapers. Re-laying the floor in our house also took a week. Later investigation revealed that the cost of new maple flooring for our house would have been in the vicinity of $900 (Fig. 6-3).

The double floor in the bathroom was of tongue and groove spruce. Here we installed a trap door, cut through both floors, to give access to the crawl space. This was necessary in order to install the plumbing and to provide entry for any future repairs (Fig. 6-4).

INSULATION

The more I investigated the pros and cons of insulation, the more confused I became, at first. It seemed as if each carpenter, contractor, or dealer that I questioned had a different point of view. Indeed, even the building code specifications have fluctuated in the last five years due to ambiguity regarding the merits and drawbacks of insulating materials and methods. After sifting through a good deal of information, I arrived at these basic concepts.

Conserving energy and heat are basic aspects of house design. Unless you live in a tropical or similar climate, some form of insulation will be necessary to conserve heat and keep the house from feeling cold. Insulation, without doubt, is effective.

The primary negative aspect of insulation that I encountered in my queries was that of condensation and rot. If not properly installed, insulation will very quickly destroy any wood it is near. I personally have seen a house, just six years old, with all its exterior wall boards so rotten and damp that it was possible to push my fingers through them.

The solution to this problem, I was told, is adequate ventilation. Outside air must be able to freely circulate on the exterior side of the insulation, thereby removing any condensation. On the inner side of the insulation, a *vapor barrier* is installed (usually plastic sheeting or a type of treated paper) to prevent any moisture inside the house from penetrating the insulation. (The source of condensation is the moisture from inside the house that is created due to cooking, washing, and everyday living. This heated moisture passes into the walls, through the insulation, and contacts the cold surface of the exterior wall where it condenses and begins the process of damp rot.)

Therefore, to use contemporary insulating materials and methods you must be sure to include in the design methods to ventilate the walls and ceilings.

Ventilation for the ceiling is accomplished by the use of attic vents or, in the case of an open interior ceiling, vents placed in the edges of eave boards. (See Fig. 4-12.) Ventilating the interior walls is done by leaving an air space between the insulation and the outside wall. This air space should then be vented to the outside via the eaves. The air space is created by the use of the proper size batts that fit between vertical 2 × 4 studs. The studs form the skeleton of the inside walls and are discussed later.

Insulating a house can also be accomplished without the use of batts or styrofoam sheets. This method makes use of the fact that a dead air space acts as an insulating medium by itself. To use this method, a space of at least 2 inches is left between the inner wall and the concrete surface of the exterior wall. A vapor barrier is placed just under-

Fig. 6-4. Completed shell of house.

neath the wall covering and fastened in place. This barrier is a heavy aluminum foil that is obtainable in large rolls from a building supplier. This is the method we chose and it has kept our house snug and warm during very cold winter temperatures (Fig. 6-5).

Other insulating techniques include the use of double- and triple-glazed windows, weather stripping, specially treated drapes and blinds that prevent heat escape through windows, burying the north wall of the house in a mound of earth, and insulating the footing.

Double-glazed windows are bought pre-built, and they are an advanced form of the storm window. Storm windows were commonplace not so many years ago and most of us remember the winter feelings that accompanied their going on in late fall. They were screwed in place on the exterior of the house, covering the existing windows. The idea was to create a dead air space between the two windows and thus an insulation effect. With the advent of permanent aluminum storm windows and double-glazed windows, storm windows have almost disappeared.

Double-glazed windows are two panes of glass in one frame separated by an air space and sealed in place. They have one disadvantage—if their seal develops a leak, condensation will form between the glass on cold days and the window will become fogged up. It is impossible to repair it so it stays as a minor source of irritation. One solution is to deliberately break the seal by drilling tiny holes between

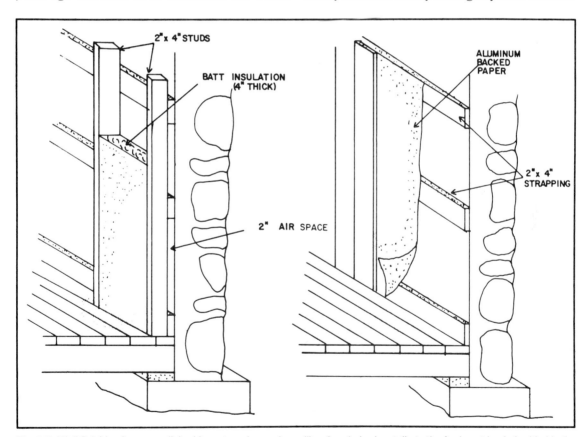

Fig. 6-5. Wall finishing is accomplished in a stone house by nailing 2 × 4s horizontally to the furring strips imbedded in the concrete. Next, insulation is installed; either aluminum building foil may be fastened directly to the 2 × 4s and then the wall covering applied, or 2 × 4 studs can be nailed to the strapping and insulation installed between them before the wall covering goes on. Both are effective but the first method is less expensive.

the two panes of glass. This permits the condensation to escape by letting the air flow in and out but in insufficient amounts to destroy the insulating effect.

There are now on the market specially made window blinds that reflect heat and are resistant to its passage. They are opened during the day and closed at night to act as insulating barriers. They seal tightly all around their perimeter and are installed in the same manner as outside storm windows.

Burying the north wall of a house in the earth is not something new. People all over the world have know for centuries about the insulating effects of digging into the ground. Witness the sod huts dug into the prairie by the early settlers to resist the cruel winters. What is new are the fascinating designs that take advantage of this old knowledge. For example, houses are being built with a north wall buried in the earth and the south wall generously exposed to the sun with many large windows. The solar heat is collected both passively and actively. Passively, by direct radiation into the house and actively, by being used to heat a vast amount of water stored in the house, releasing heat during the night. This stored heat is distributed throughout the house by fans or a blower system. This heat, plus the insulation of the earth and other types of insulation, makes the heating costs very low indeed.

Insulating the footing is a proven method of saving on heating costs. This is done by placing rigid styrofoam insulation all around the outside perimeter of the footing to a depth that is below the frost line. The styrofoam is placed directly against the footing and backfilled with earth. The heat in the basement or crawl space is then retained and does not escape through the concrete walls.

With all these methods we are now seeing the phenomena of the super insulated house. In some of these houses, the insulation is very thick and drafts are non-existent. The result is a sort of oven effect. The inhabitants suffer from a variety of ailments such as dry skin, respiratory problems, colds and sinus irritations, headaches, and so on. They have to buy a humidifier or leave windows open for a change of air which, it seems to us, defeats the purpose of their abundant insulation.

The answer, we think, lies somewhere in between and is ultimately up to the builder to decide upon. Take time to investigate your requirements and the possible solutions. Perhaps you will create a unique new method to add to the mainstream of ideas.

WARM AIR CIRCULATION

Recirculating warm air trapped at ceiling level is another method whereby heat conservation is achieved. Two methods used to create an air flow within a house (in the winter) are to push the hot air down from the ceilings, or to suck the cold air up from the floor. Both are accomplished by the use of fans. These fans use very little electricity and are designed to provide a steady, soft flowing current of air to recycle the heat and eliminate hot spots.

Large ceiling fans are popular with many people. These rotate at variable speeds that are controlled by the twist of a switch and come in various colors and designs. (I never see one without thinking of Humphrey Bogart and Sydney Greenstreet.) These fans push large amounts of hot air downward to create an air flow. They are popular in big department stores.

The method we chose was to install a wooden tube about 1 foot square, that ran from floor to ceiling in the central part of the house. We concealed it as part of a partition. At the top, it opens into our loft. At the bottom of the tube are metal vents, and inside the tube near the top is a small electric fan. When in operation the fan sucks the cool air from the floor through the vents, up the tube and towards the roof. This forces the hot air at the peak to flow downward and establishes an even air flow. This system is inexpensive and only required the purchase of a small fan motor ($15). The large ceiling fans begin around $100 (Fig. 6-6). We find that we only use the fan on the coldest days and the rest of the time it is not needed.

I made the fan blade by cutting out a circular piece of metal 8 inches in diameter. Then I cut and shaped the blades to create the fan effect. The fan was attached to the shaft of the small motor using a

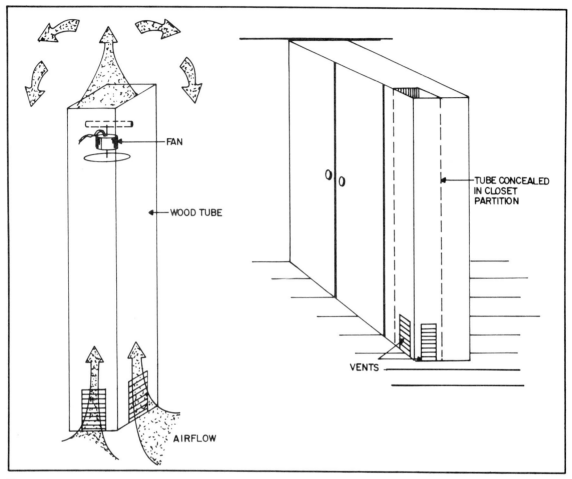

Fig. 6-6. Recirculation of warm air that is trapped at ceiling level conserves energy. We installed a small fan in a wooden tube that reached from the floor to the loft. When in operation, the fan draws air from floor level and blows it upwards toward the peak of the roof. The warm air is forced down as a result and replaced by cooler air that also serves to keep the loft at a livable temperature. The tube is in a partition and has metal vents at its base.

special nut that is easily purchased at a hardware store. To make the fan run as silently as possible within the wooden shaft, it was suspended from a nylon line stretched across the top opening. The electrical cord from the motor ran down the shaft and plugged into a socket equipped with an on/off switch. When in operation, the fan draws the air from the bottom vents and projects it towards the peak of the roof, forcing a displacement of warm air trapped there. It is possible to reverse the process and draw the warm air down and blow it out the floor vents but we chose the former system since it

serves to cool the loft whenever we use it as sleeping space for friends or guests (Fig. 6-7).

FRAMING

The framing can be viewed as the interior skeletal structure for the walls and partitions. All the framing was done with 2 × 4 lumber—a common method. Framing is usually erected on 16-inch centers, which means the vertical studs (2 × 4's) are spaced 16 inches apart. A standard stud size is a piece of 2 × 4 that is 8 feet long. These studs are

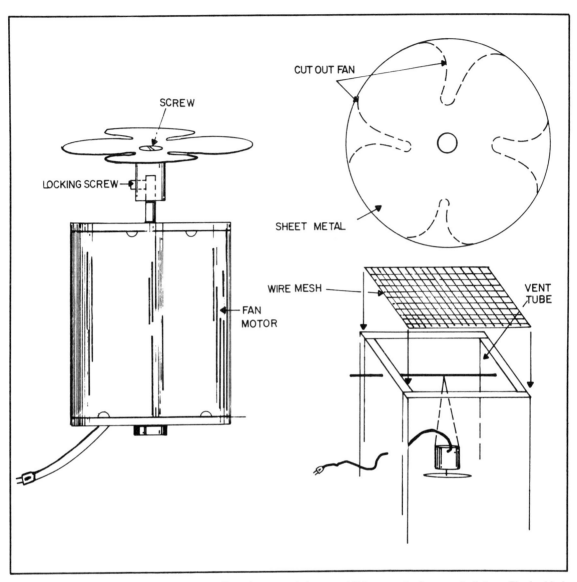

Fig. 6-7. The fan used to recirculate the warm ceiling air was made from an old blower motor for a small oil stove. The fan blade was cut from a piece of sheet metal and bent to form a fan shape. The whole mechanism was suspended from a nylon line inside the top of the wooden tube, reducing fan noise to a minimum.

sold by building suppliers and can be priced separately or by the 1000 b.f. If you design your house with this in mind, you will not be in difficulty by having to deal with non-standard sizes. For example, plywood and gypsum board sheets are sold in 4 × 8-foot sheets, as is wall paneling. This complements the 8-foot studding and wall framing. If your

walls are 8½ feet high and, if you use these materials, a lot of cutting will be involved.

Nails

Framing used to be nailed together using 4-inch common spikes. These nails were smooth and relatively stout and very often split the 2 × 4 lumber. A new type of nail has been in use for the past several years—the *spiral nail*. It is sold commercially under different brand names but they are all essentially the same. These nails look just as though someone held them by both ends and twisted them a few times, which is exactly what has been done during their manufacture. When one of these nails is driven into a piece of wood, it rotates much like a screw and is therefore less likely to split it. The resulting holding power is greatly increased due to this twist, and the nail can be made thinner than a common nail. These spiral nails are available in all sizes for boarding a floor, nailing rafters and framing, roofing, and so on. Their only disadvantage, if you could call it one, appears if you make a mistake in nailing. Withdrawing one of these nails, especially a 4-inch spike, will very effectively demonstrate their holding power.

Another very useful type of nail is the *scaffold nail*. This is a double headed nail used for building temporary structures such as bracing, staging, wooden forms, etc. The nail is driven into a piece of wood until the first head is snug. Upon removal, the second head, spaced about ¼-inch from the first, is easily gripped by your hammer or wrecking bar. These nails are very useful and we used them constantly.

Nail sizes can cause confusion if they are listed in *pennies*. A 10d nail means a 10 penny nail and is a term that was common usage in years past. The early settlers did not have the luxury of nails to build their houses and barns. Instead, they fastened everything with wooden pegs driven into holes bored with a hand drill called an *auger*. Iron nails appeared with the blacksmiths who made them by hand, using forges and anvils. These flat, square edged nails were sold so many for a penny. When steel nails became available the term "penny" was kept and designated by the letter "d." Thus, 10d means a 3-inch common steel nail. "Common" designates a standard, straight nail used for all-purpose work. It is not galvanized, ribbed, spiraled, or wedged as are other special purpose nails. The "d" sizes range from 2d to 60d, with the 2d to 16d increasing in length in ¼-inch increments. Above 16d, they grow longer in ½-inch increments.

Example: 6d = 2″, 8d = 2½″, 10d = 3″, 16d = 3½″, and 20d = 4″.

There are many types of special purpose nails that are used for specific purposes. You must be aware of this, because the dealer doesn't always take the time to explain. He assumes that you know what you want. For example, galvanized steel roofing requires a special galvanized nail with a lead washer. This nail seals tightly when driven through the roofing because the washer becomes moulded around the nail head. It also has a very sharp point for piercing the metal and is heavier, to resist bending. Asphalt shingles require a nail with a large flat head. These nails are ribbed to hold tightly in the roofing boards. There are special nails for gypsum board, cedar shingles, hardwood flooring, wall paneling, and so on. Make sure you have the correct nail for the job at hand. Improper nails can ruin your efforts.

Partitions and Wall Coverings

The framing in a stone house will be attached to the floor, the ceiling (if trusses are used), and the walls. To attach the framing to the walls, 2 × 4's are first nailed horizontally to the furring strips imbedded in the concrete (Fig. 6-8). These horizontal 2 × 4s are placed at the top mid-point and bottom of the walls (Fig. 6-9). Then, according to your design, the vertical framing is erected. Our vertical framing outlined three paritions that doubled as closets and shelves. Ordinary wall paritions are about 6 inches thick. Two of our partitions are 24 inches thick and serve as closets. The top of our bedroom/bathroom partition serves as a support for the tie beam that is part of the loft floor. The floor joists for the loft consist of 6 × 6-inch beams that rest on this partition in the middle and on the wall plates on either end. Thus the north third of our house is loft area and the south two-thirds has an open ceiling (Fig. 6-10).

When the framing is completed, the next step is the installation of plumbing, wiring, and insulation. (Plumbing and wiring are discussed in the following chapters.) Insulation can be installed either in batts or using the aluminum paper method.

Fig. 6-8. Working on the interior. No stove made-the fur hat a must.

Both are suited to the stud framework. Rigid foam may also be used but spacers should be installed to keep an air space between the foam and the concrete wall. Over the batt insulation, a vapor barrier is stapled in place, covering completely the inside of the exterior walls. (Insulation is not placed in interior wall partitions, although I have heard of this error being made.)

The wall covering goes over the insulation. If you are using gypsum board, it is cut to fit and nailed in place. Likewise wall paneling. Don't forget all the openings that will have to be carefully measured to accommodate the electrical and plumbing fittings. Trim will go around all windows and doors.

This trim is usually made of wood that has been cut in different shapes called moulding. Moulding is added to complete the interior finish and serves to cover the gaps between the walls and ceilings, walls and floor, and doors and windows. Many types are available and the best solution is to ask the dealer what is available, unless you make your own.

Our walls were simply done. We omitted batt insulation and stapled building paper to the 2 × 4 strapping attached to the furring strips. We then nailed 1-inch planed hemlock boards vertically to the 2 × 4 strapping. To cover the cracks where two boards butted against each other, we nailed on strips of wood, *(battens)*. These were 1½ inches wide and ⅜-inch thick, beveled on both outside edges. They were cut on our bench saw from 1-inch boards. The wall boards were cut to fit between the floor and the slope of the roof. A piece of ½ × 2-inch trim covered the joints between the wall boards and roof. This gave the 2 inches of dead air space all around the house between the wall boards and the concrete. Our interior partitions were covered in the same fashion (Fig. 6-11).

Using solid wood as a wall covering not only looks pleasing but it has its own insulating effect. Also, since we had our own logs, the cost was low. We did compare costs, though, to determine the market value of each type of wall covering. The

prices of each, to cover 1000 square feet of wall, when bought from a supplier would have been as follows:

¼-inch Douglas fir plywood, good-one-side: $510
½-inch gypsum board (plus crack filling): $235
⅛-inch wall paneling: $250
1-inch lumber (planed one side): $240

From this, it can be seen that wood is competitive in price and plywood is by far the most expensive. The price of wood rises when the wood

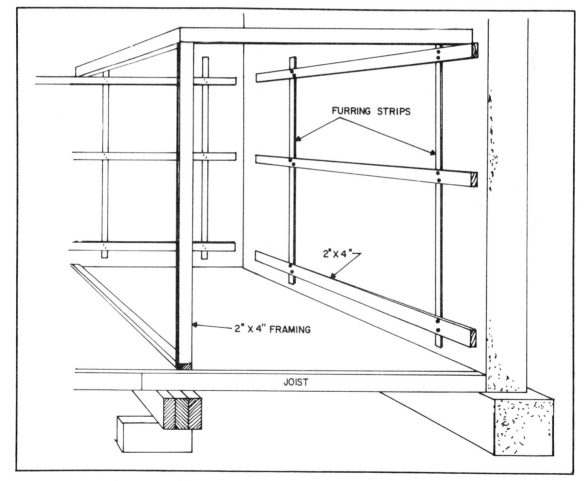

Fig. 6-9. The framing for the inside of the house uses furring strips and horizontal strapping. Using them as a base to nail the interior studs on, the framing of the partitions and closets was erected according to plan.

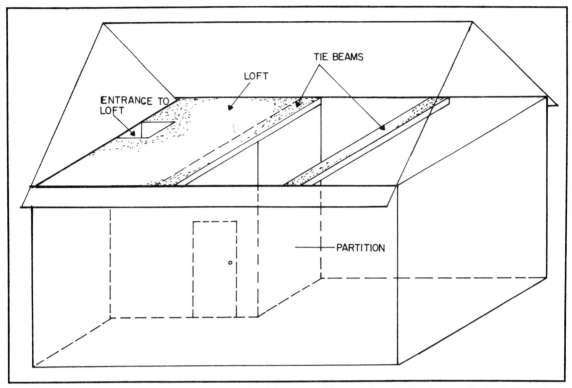

Fig. 6-10. A loft was buit using a tie beam as part of the floor joist system. The rest of the floor joists were attached to the plate on either end and supported in the middle by the room partition below. The entrance to the left was against the back wall, via an oak ladder.

you choose is imported or if it is specially edged, as in tongue and groove or shiplap. There are other options available if you prefer wood. Old barn boards, silver in color from years of exposure to the weather, have become quite popular. They give a room a unique look that cannot be duplicated with paneling. If you wish to use old boards of any type inside your house, however, be absolutely certain they don't harbor any forms of life such as termites or woodworms. (This type of wall covering has become so popular that a service has sprung up to fumigate the lumber and sand blast the surface to remove dirt and moss.)

Other choices include shingling the interior wall with wood shingles, covering it with glued-on material such as burlap, and a revival of the old methods of plastering and *stippling*. (Stippling is applying a kind of plaster to make a wall look like a pond covered with little wavelets and points.)

KITCHEN AND BATHROOM

We considered many alternatives when choosing a design for our kitchen cupboards. Our final choice was to have open shelving above the sink and counter top, and doors below. We found cupboard doors a constant nuisance in our farmhouse so we decided to eliminate them in our new house. We can now view our collection of pottery dishes and find it an attractive feature. We also do not tend to clutter the shelves by storing unused items on them, which is easily done behind closed doors.

The shelving and doors were made of hemlock boards that have a beautiful grain and are a pinkish color. The counter top was made of 2-inch oak planks glued together edgewise, sanded, and finished to show the natural color and grain. The oak came from a large tree on our woodlot. The doors for the bottom cupboard were simply constructed by fastening two hemlock boards together

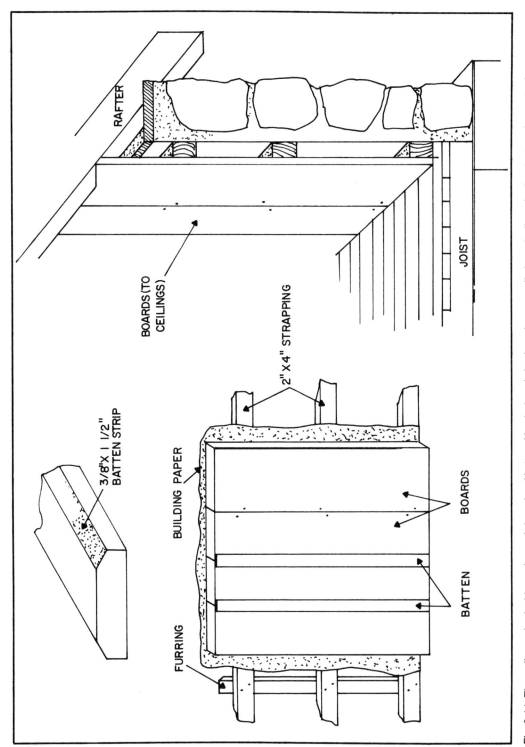

Fig. 6-11. The wall covering inside our house is board and batten. Hemlock and pine boards were nailed vertically to the 2 × 4 strapping and a batten was cut from 1-inch lumber. To make the batten, strips 1½ inches wide and ⅜-inch thick were cut and beveled on two edges. They were then nailed over the joins between the wall boards. The boards extended to the sloped roof, where they were finished with a narrow strip of wood that covered the join between board and roof.

In the diagram, the following labels appear: RAFTER, BOARDS (TO CEILINGS), JOIST, 2" X 4" STRAPPING, 3/8"X 1 1/2" BATTEN STRIP, BUILDING PAPER, BOARDS, FURRING, BATTEN.

111

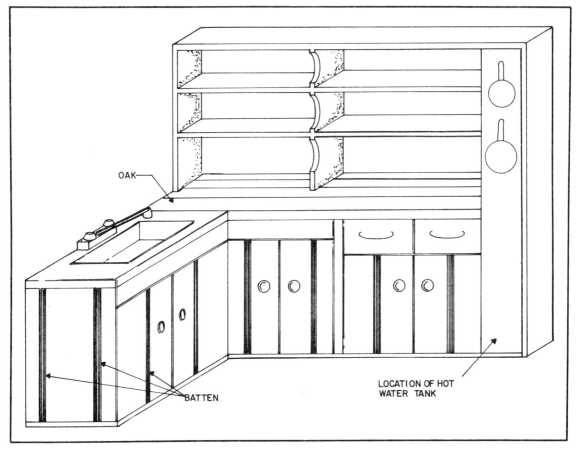

OAK

BATTEN

LOCATION OF HOT
WATER TANK

Fig. 6-12. Kitchen cabinets of hemlock and oak. We preferred open shelving above the counter top and doors below. The single sink was inlaid in the oak counter by cutting a hole with a jigsaw. Doors were made in the board and batten style and the hot water tank was concealed within a small end closet.

using 1 × 3-inch cleats on the inside. The crack between the boards was covered with a 1-inch batten and matched the wall style. Drawers were made using hemlock boards, but oak was used for the runners. The completed unit was simple, functional, and aesthetically pleasing (Fig. 6-12).

The price of pre-built kitchen cabinets begins around $1000 and can easily soar to $6000 and beyond. This is without the sink and fittings. Our cost was approximately $100 and this included the proverbial kitchen sink.

The bathroom was finished with board and batten walls and a tongue and groove floor. We located a large cast iron sink (7 × 20 × 30) that was covered with porcelain and in excellent shape that

the owner gave us free. We built the sink into an oak cabinet and above it placed a large mirror in an oak frame. (The oak still coming from that same large tree.) We then bought a bathtub for $40 from people who were renovating their house. It was also cast iron, covered with white enamel and sat on four small legs. It suits the wood theme of the floor and walls admirably. The toilet was obtained from another house undergoing modifications. The total cost of outfitting our bathroom with fixtures was $75. Since we built our house, we have run across all sorts of bargains for a variety of articles. Windows, lumber, plumbing and wiring supplies, all at substantial savings and in excellent condition. They are as near as the classified ads.

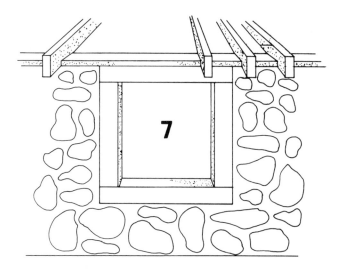

Plumbing and Heating

WITH AN UNDERSTANDING OF THE PRINCIPLES involved in a plumbing system, you can do all of the work yourself. These principles must be followed for the system to work properly and for the protection of your health. If your plumbing is going to be connected to a water and sewage system of a town or city, then your work is considerably simplified. In the country or where a sewer system is non-existent, then another method is employed. This is the *septic system*. It provides safe disposal of all the liquid waste from your sinks, bathtub, and toilet.

Providing that your site is approved for the installation of a septic system by your local health department, then you are permitted to do all the work yourself, subject to inspection by the same department. A standard procedure for building your system is as follows: a large tank is installed near the house into which the effluents from the house will flow. From the tank, waste water is fed into a network of piping designed to diffuse it over a large area of ground where it will be absorbed. This is termed the *disposal bed* or *field*. The ability of your soil to absorb and disperse water is measurable and called its rate of percolation (see Chapter 1).

The tank should be built of concrete or fiberglass and never of metal, which would decay in the ground. The tank traps and holds sewage, which is then broken down by bacterial action. The disposal bed promotes even filtration of the resulting effluent, reducing chances of bacteria entering any water supply (Fig. 7-1). The dimensions of the tank and disposal bed will depend on the type of soil, the amount of sewage and drainage to be disposed of, and your local bylaws.

The interior plumbing system is designed in relation to the septic tank system because within the septic system, specifically the tank, gases are generated by the biological action of the decomposing sewage. These gases are noxious and explosive and they must be vented into the air and dispersed. They must not be allowed to enter the house via the drain pipes. A system is used whereby the tank is vented back through the house to an opening above the roof. This is called a *stack vent* system. It serves two purposes: the gases flow

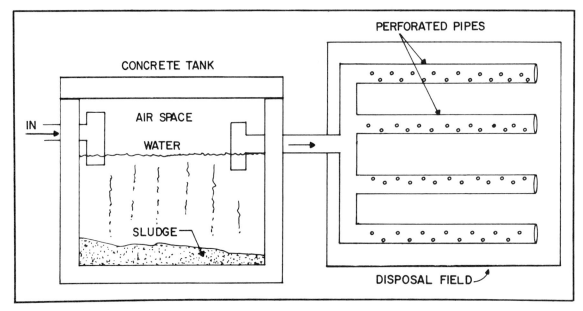

Fig. 7-1. A basic septic system consists of a tank and disposal bed. The fiberglass or concrete tank traps waste material and passes on the waste water to a network of perforated pipes, which disperse it into the ground. Within the tank, bacterial action dissolves waste matter.

from the tank to be dispersed above roof level and the stack provides the necessary air intake to the drainage system to prevent vacuum problems when water is exiting the house.

This vacuum action occurs when water flows down a pipe. It pushes air before it, thereby sucking air behind it. This air must come from somewhere in the system and if it is not provided by a stack vent, then it will draw it from elsewhere. Usually "elsewhere" is another sink or bathtub drain. When this happens the water drains away with a pulsing motion and you hear sucking and gurgling noises coming from other sinks or the bathtub. Thus you must plan the layout of your stack vent and allow for the various pipes branching from it to drain and vent the sinks, tub, and toilet. This is the *drainage system,* and it is separate and distinct from the *supply pipe* system.

Figure 7-2 shows a basic drainage system. In addition to the stack vent, each sink, tub, etc. has an S-shaped pipe underneath its drain. This is called a *trap,* and its purpose is to hold a quantity of water at all times, which effectively blocks gas from the septic tank on its route to the roof.

The supply system of piping includes the line incoming from the well to the pump and pipes that distribute the hot and cold water to sinks, bath, toilet, and hot water tank. This system is divided into the hot and cold lines. From the pump, cold water is fed directly to all the cold water taps in the house, to the toilet, to the hot water heating tank, and to any other outlets such as an outside hose connection. Hot water, which is supplied by the hot water tank, is fed to all the hot water taps plus any special outlets that may be required, such as radiator heating.

To keep the cost of your plumbing system down, it is a good idea to plan to make your complete plumbing system as compact as possible. For example, if you have a two-story house, try to arrange any upstairs plumbing to be directly above downstairs plumbing. Long, expensive runs of pipe are thus avoided along with the labor involved of routing it within the walls.

For a bungalow-type house, such as ours, the kitchen and bathroom plumbing should be adjacent to one another if possible. Figure 7-3 shows the layout of our plumbing, mainly in the northeast

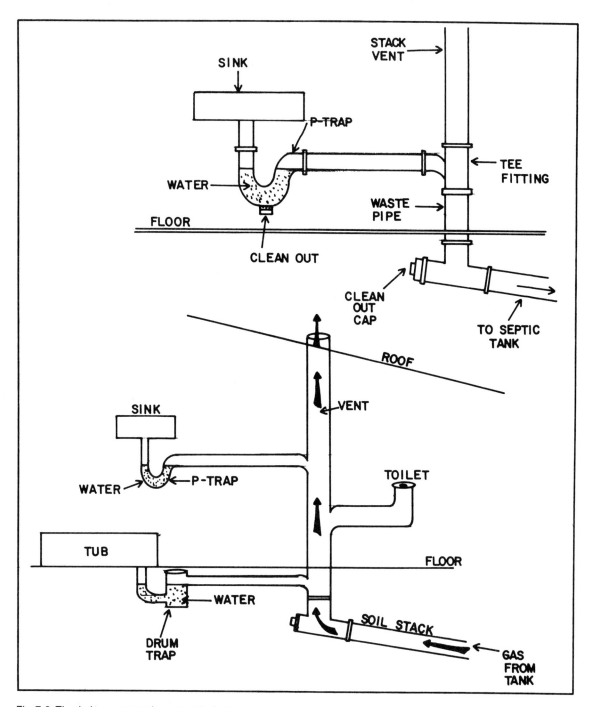

Fig. 7-2. The drainage system is a network of pipes designed to drain household water into the septic tank or sewage system of a town or city. Small pipes from each tub and sink are fed into a larger pipe, called a stack, which rises vertically to exit through the roof. The stack admits air for the easy drainage of water and vents gases from the septic tank. P-traps are attached to each unit to prevent these gases from passing into the house.

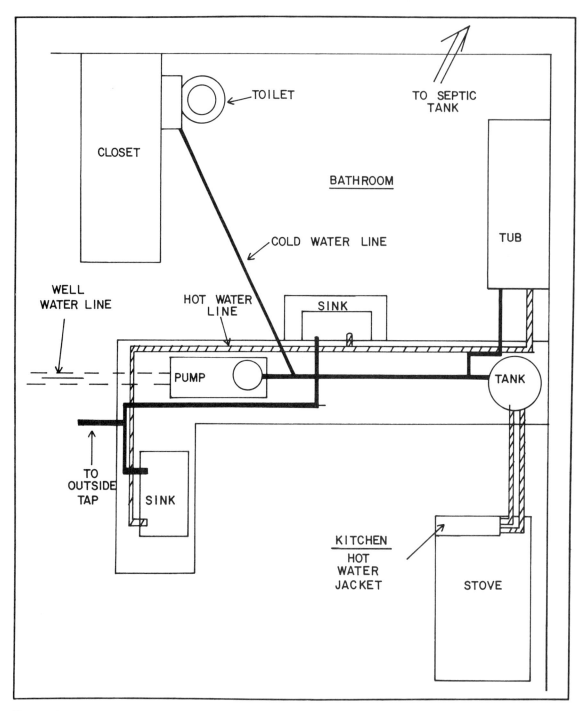

Fig. 7-3. The supply system of piping draws water from well or town water supply and distributes it throughout the house. Cold water is fed directly to the taps, toilet, etc., but hot water is heated and stored before distribution. Cold water line may be plastic pipe, but copper is used for hot.

section of the house. (Of course, if you plan to have hot water heating throughout your house, then your system will necessarily be spread throughout the complete house.)

While the system is being built, it is a good idea to wrap the hot water pipes with insulation designed for this purpose. It will prevent any unnecessary heat loss from these pipes and reduce your costs for heating hot water. Likewise, the tank used to store the hot water is usually insulated, but if, like us, you heat your water with wood heat, then you will have to insulate your tank yourself.

All the piping for the supply and drainage systems must be concealed within the walls and under the floor of the house, which is why the plumbing is done when the framing is completed. The piping installed at this time is called the *rough plumbing* and includes the stack vent and all the supply and drain pipes. The *finish plumbing* is done when the interior walls are complete and includes the sinks, tub, taps, toilet, pump, etc.

MATERIALS

Plumbing has been considerably simplified by modern technology to the point where the home owner can do most of the plumbing jobs with complete confidence in the results. To facilitate this new awareness, do-it-yourself plumbing supply shops have sprung up all over the country. At these establishments a novice plumber walks in, states his intentions, either with or without any formal knowledge, and a helpful clerk will supply any needed information along with the suitable parts. I don't know how this is affecting the plumbing fraternity but I suspect that often there are distress calls sent out by home owners knee-deep in watery basements. With a grasp of the fundamentals and the proper tools, however, the owner-builder can expect 100 percent success with the installation of a basic system.

The tools needed include a hacksaw, propane torch, solder, glue, pipe cutter for copper pipes, pipe wrench, and an assortment of pliers and basic carpentry tools. The use of each will be described as we go along.

The piping used is either plastic or metal. For the drainage systems, plastic pipe is used. (Copper

is reserved for the hot and cold water systems.) Plastic pipe is of two types: rigid and flexible, both available in various diameters. Within the plumbing system there are pipes that carry no pressure, as in the drainage pipes; and pipes with pressure, the hot and cold water supply. Thus, the pipes also have a rating—their *psi rate*.

Note that psi means pounds per square inch and indicates the force with which the water presses against the inside of the pipe. A rating of 75 psi means that above that water pressure, the pipe will likely burst. The average pressure of a pump system varies between 30 to 50 psi, and a town or city water system can go as high as 100 pis, depending on the location of house in relation to the pumping station. The closer you live to this pumping station, the higher your water pressure and vice versa.

When you buy a pump, the psi will be indicated in the pump's specifications and you will buy pipe accordingly. The pipe that comes from the well is generally flexible plastic pipe with a low pressure rating, since there is no substantial force involved in drawing the water. A good size pipe for this purpose is 1-inch in diameter, and a good quality pipe is preferable. Cheaper pipe has thinner walls, is easily crushed, and will kink if bent. When laying the line from the well to the house, a good practice is to insert the 1-inch pipe in a larger pipe before covering it over. We placed our 1-inch pipe inside lengths of 2-inch rigid pipe to protect it from the weight of the earth. The pipe must be buried deep enough so it won't freeze. It enters the house under the footing, through the hole you hopefully remembered to install.

The flexible piping comes in rolls, usually of 50 to 100 feet in length. Diameters are available from ½-, ¾-, 1-, 1¼-, 1½-inch etc., up to 3-inch. It is sold either in a full roll or per foot, depending where you buy it. It also comes in different qualities and usually the cheap, bargain pipe is not worth it in the long term. Flexible pipe is connected by the use of clamps and small rigid plastic connectors. To join two sections of pipe, for example, a solid connector is inserted inside one piece of pipe and then the other. Both connections are secured with an adjustable clamp and a screwdriver.

Rigid plastic pipe is also available in various grades, lengths, and diameters. Since this pipe is used mainly for drainage systems, pressure considerations don't usually apply. There is a type of rigid plastic pipe used for pressure systems and for hot water. They are intended as an alternative to copper pipe but, in my experience, it hasn't found much favor among the plumbers with which I spoke, It is not as solid and durable as copper and is difficult to repair.)

The rigid plastic piping we used is very easy to work. To cut a piece of pipe, all that is needed is a hacksaw. To join two pieces together, merely clean the ends with a special liquid cleaner, apply the proper glue and push the joints tight. It sets in 10 minutes and can be used after 24 hours. There are a multitude of connections available to facilitate the construction of any plumbing job, incguding 90° elbows, 45° elbows, adapters, T-couplings, P-traps, and so on (Fig. 7-4). All the piping used for our waste system and septic field was rigid plastic; the waste pipe 4 inches in diameter and the perforated septic field pipe 3 inches. The pipe used for the vent system and sink drains was 1½ inches in diameter.

We used ½-inch copper pipe for both the cold and hot water supply systems. Although it's not a necessity to use copper for the cold water lines, we preferred it because it is much more durable than plastic, has a higher psi rating and, when properly assembled, has tighter joints. Copper pipe is available in different diameters from ¼-inch up to 3-inch or more. At one time some houses used copper for all the plumbing pipes but the cost of copper has steadily risen to the point where it is no longer feasible, unless you have unlimited funds. The standard size for water lines is ½-inch and most of the fittings available are this size. As with plastic pipe, the copper is sold in different grades, thin skinned and thick skinned. The heavy pipe is preferable but the thinner will do under ordinary circumstances.

It is best to buy new copper pipe and fittings because old pipe sometimes has deteriorated and, if there is old solder on the connections, it is next to useless to use because it will leak 98 percent of the time. Old copper pipe that has been frozen with water inside it is also useless since it will have been stretched by the pressure from the ice, and the fittings won't fit the enlarged diameter. Unless you measure this kind of pipe with calipers, it is very difficult to see any appreciable difference in size. So, if buying secondhand pipe, be sure of its condition. We were fortunate and obtained a large amount of our required copper pipe secondhand and in excellent condition.

The technique for fastening copper pipe is very simple yet can be extremely vexing if not approached with patience. It is absolutely necessary that the pipes and fittings to be joined are perfectly clean, with no trace of dirt or grease left on them. Otherwise, when you have finished the assembly and charge the system with water under pressure, there will be a profusion of leaky joints that are most difficult to repair.

To join copper pipe you will need a propane torch, solder and flux, and employ a technique called *sweat soldering*. The procedure is as follows:

• Measure your length of pipe and cut it with a pipe cutter. (Don't use a hacksaw because it leaves a ragged edge that is not conducive to good joints. A pipe cutter is a tool that grips the pipe and is rotated around the pipe's circumference. A sharp wheel bites into the soft metal and makes a clean edged cut through the pipe.)

• Clean the end of the pipe about 1½ inches in width and also clean the inside of the fitting that is to be attached. First, sand them with a piece of emery cloth or fine sandpaper until they are shiny. Clean both ends of the fitting. Next, finish the cleaning by polishing with a rag dipped in alcohol. Be sure that you don't touch the cleaned parts with dirty fingers.

• Using a screwdriver or a clean popsicle stick, apply flux to the cleaned sections. Flux is a brownish paste, much like grease, that is sold in small tins. The purpose of flux is to create a chemical reaction when heated that forms a strong bond between the copper and the solder. Without the flux, the joint will not be secure. Different metals require different fluxes. For copper, the flux is

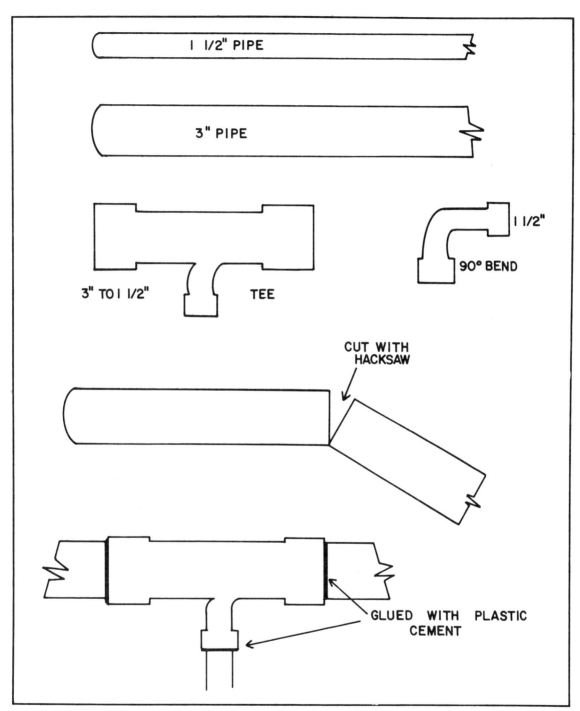

Fig. 7-4. Rigid plastic pipe is used for the drainage and venting system. Standard usage is 1½-inch pipe for sink drains, 3- or 4-inch pipe for the stack, and 3-inch perforated for the disposal bed. A hacksaw will cut it, and it is joined using a special glue. It sets in 10 minutes and can be used within 24 hours.

ammonium chloride or zinc chloride.

● Next, the pieces are heated using the propane torch. If the pipe is a long section you can hold it with your hand but, for short sections and for fittings, the holding is done with pliers. Light the torch and place the pipe end in the flame about 1½ inches from the mouth of the torch. Rotate the pipe to achieve even heating and when the flux boils and bubbles, apply the solder. (The solder used is a combination of lead and tin in a 50/50 proportion.

There are many types of solders for different jobs, but this type is all that's required for copper lines. The solder is a solid wire about 1/16-inch thick and wound on a spool. We used one spool for all our plumbing.)

● When the solder melts, it will flow all around the cleaned section of the pipe. Apply only enough to give an even coating of shiny solder and then remove the pipe from the flame and let it cool. Do the same for the inside of the fitting on both

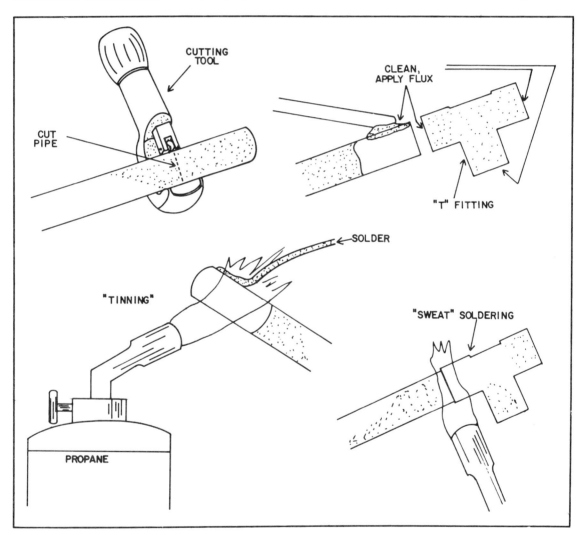

Fig. 7-5. Copper pipe is used for lines that will carry water pressure or hot water. It is connected by cutting with a proper tool and then soldering the joints. The joints are cleaned, covered with a thin skin of solder, and then fastened together in the flame of a torch—sweat soldering.

ends. This process of coating the copper with a skin of solder is called *tinning*.

- The sections of pipe and fitting are now tinned and ready to be joined together. To do this, hold them, one piece in each hand and alternately heat them in the torch flame. When they both begin to melt the skin of solder, push them firmly together while still in the flame. When they are together, remove them from the flame and, without joining the connection in any way, let it cool. You can speed this up by blowing on the joint (Fig. 7-5).

The process of sweat soldering gives solid, clean joints. As the assembly becomes more complicated, you will have to work between studs, under floors, and so on. The process is the same. Clean the joints, tin the pipe and fittings, and sweat them together. When you must work near combustible materials, use a heat shield for protection. This is a piece of metal placed between the flame and any exposed surface. When you have to solder near another connection and you don't want to loosen the already soldered joint due to the heat, wrap cold, wet cloths around the pipe to protect it.

An alternate method of soldering connections is done by eliminating the tinning step and fastening the joints together when they are cleaned and fluxed. Heat is applied to the joint and, when the flux is bubbling, the solder is applied directly to the hot metal. The solder will melt and flow into the joint by capillary action. Never melt solder with the flame; always do so by touching it to the hot metal. Do not apply too much solder to the joint. Any excess can be wiped away with a cloth, making sure not to disturb the connection. This method of direct soldering is especially useful when working on a difficult section of line such as in a corner or under a sink, etc.

You proceed until all your connections are made and the system is complete. Finally, the moment of truth, when you switch on your pump and the lines fill with water at about 45 psi. First you notice a trickle of water where that 90° elbow goes under the sink. It quickly becomes a fine spray, shooting out for a foot or more. You have a leak. If you only have one leak, you deserve congratulations for achieving 90 percent success.

Repairing that leak is done as follows:

- Drain the system completely. If a pipe contains water it will stubbornly refuse to heat up enough to melt solder.
- Heat the solder joint with a torch and break the connection.
- *Thoroughly* clean both the pipe and the fitting.
- Apply flux, reheat, and add a little solder.
- Sweat them together and let cool before recharging the system.

(Another way to attempt a repair is to drain the system, heat the joint, and apply solder directly over the leak. Sometimes it will work. Many times it won't and you will have a big mess with globs of solder sticking to the pipe oozing water.)

Working with copper pipe is not at all difficult, although it may seem so at first. Try practicing a few joints first to get the feel. Don't overheat the pipe when tinning or sweating it. Don't try to manipulate a joint while it is cooling. Always take your time. These tips will ensure a more successful result.

SEPTIC SYSTEM

The septic system begins outside the house. A large 4-inch pipe, which will carry all the waste water and sewage, runs from the house to the tank. This pipe must be sloped to facilitate the flow of water and solids. Too much slope and the water will flow away too fast, leaving behind waste solids that will, in time, clog up the pipe. Too little slope or pitch and the water will not flow at all. The standard pitch for the waste pipe is ¼ inch per foot. Thus for a 12-foot run of pipe, the tank end would be 3 inches lower than the house end. The pipe used is 4-inch rigid plastic (Fig. 7-6).

Where the pipe enters and exits the tank, T-fittings are installed as shown in Fig. 7-1. The exit fitting is lower than the entrance so that the tank acts as a trap and the water cannot back up the pipe. Due to bacterial action within the tank, toxic gases are given off and these must be released. The gases enter the top of the T-fitting to be vented into the open air via the stack vent.

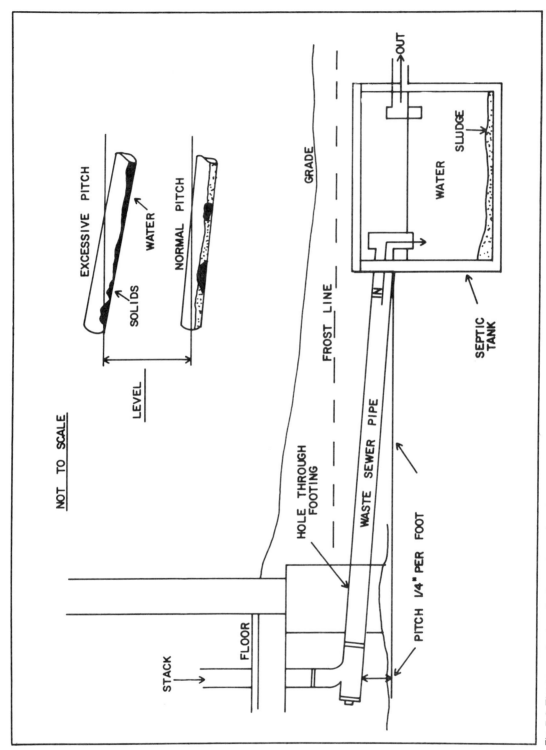

Fig. 7-6. The sewer pipe from the house to septic tank must be sloped to move waste material. The pitch must be neither too excessive nor too shallow. A pitch of ¼-inch per horizontal foot of travel is a standard specification.

The tank and the piping are buried underground and the effluent from the tank is fed to a disposal bed or septic field. The pipe from the tank is connected to several lengths of 3-inch perforated pipes, which are also below ground. Ditches are dug, partially filled with gravel, the pipe installed and then covered over with more gravel. (The lengths and sizes of the ditches depend upon the local bylaws and the size of your system.)

If the land you are building on doesn't disperse water very well, then you may have to build a raised septic field. Gravel is laid directly on top of the soil and then the piping. Over this goes more gravel and then a layer of topsoil. Again, the size is determined by the bylaws and so on. This method can be very

costly since the gravel has to be trucked in and 50 to 100 loads at $20 per load soon adds up (Fig. 7-7).

To build our tank, we dug a hole to the required depth, about 6 feet, and erected wooden forms for the bottom slab of the tank. The concrete was poured directly on the hard clay to a depth of 5 inches forming a slab 4 foot × 6 foot × 5 inches. After the slab was hardened, wooden forms spaced 4 inches apart were erected for the walls. The forms were made of 1 inch lumber and built so that the walls could be made in one pour. We installed short lengths of 4 inch pipe in the forms to which we could later make our connections to the house and septic field. With the walls completed, we made a concrete top (Fig. 7-8).

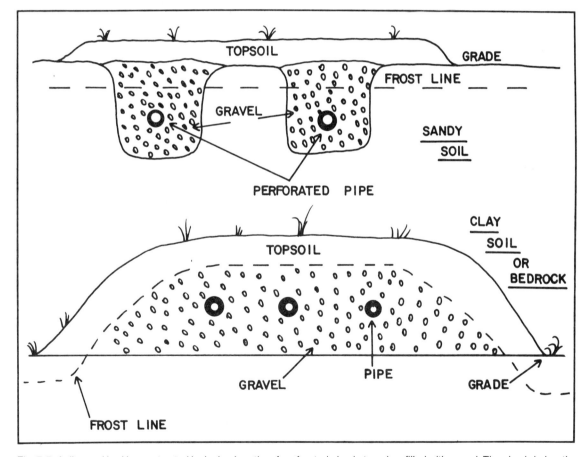

Fig. 7-7. A disposal bed is constructed by laying lengths of perforated pipe in trenches filled with gravel. The pipe is below the frost line. For a site with shallow soil or bedrock, a disposal bed must be built by hauling in gravel and earth until the required depth is achieved. The pipes are laid as shown and the dispersal effect is thus above the original grade level.

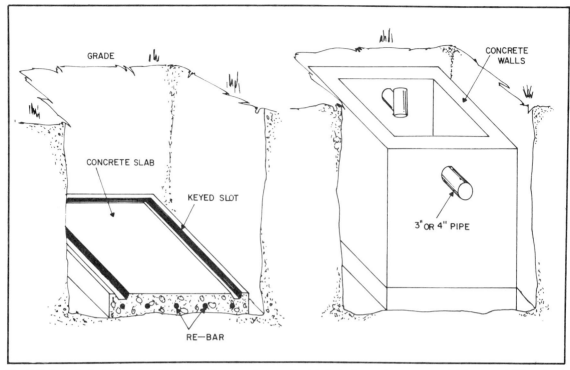

Fig. 7-8. A septic tank is made with wooden forms and concrete. A hole is dug and a concrete slab is poured. When hard, wooden forms are built on the slab and the walls are poured. Holes are left to accommodate the entry and exit piping. Note the keyed slot in the concrete slab to firmly anchor the walls.

Because of the weight factor we made the top in three sections. Each section was poured in a 2-foot × 4-foot × 4-inch shallow wooden frame that we sat on a flat base. One-half-inch iron bars were embedded lengthwise in the wet concrete. This greatly strengthens the concrete and prevents the completed section from cracking in two. Heavy wire was also embedded in the wet concrete and wrapped around the bars to provide handles; very handy later on when the heavy slabs are moved into position. The sections were then placed side by side on top of the tank (Fig. 7-9). Over the top of the tank we shoveled a 2-inch layer of earth and seeded it with grass seed.

The pipe that ran directly from the tank was a solid 4-inch pipe. This pipe ran for a distance of 15 feet before it branched into a network of 3-inch rigid perforated pipe. The perforated pipe was laid in trenches and encased in gravel, as previously mentioned. The holes in the pipe are all on one side and

are placed face down to ensure drainage. The solid side prevents entry of any dirt into the pipe, which would clog it. Once the pipe is covered over, a layer of earth is shoveled in place, and grass seed sown.

Depending upon the amount of use your system will be subject to, it should operate trouble-free for several years. After that time the tank will be filled with accumulated sludge and need to be cleaned out. The old method was to take the top off the tank and dip it out using buckets. Fortunately, there is a septic tank cleaning service that sends a large truck to clean your tank by pumping the sludge into the holding tank on the truck. It is then taken away. You must open the septic tank yourself, however, or be charged extra for that service.

Problems do arise with septic systems and a major one is filling up too fast with sludge. This is due to draining all the household waste into one tank. A septic tank is designed to receive the waste from the toilet and hold it in one spot where biologic action will cause decay of the material. A septic tank is alive with these bacteria, or it should be. When the waste water from the sink and tub arrives in the tank, it carries with it the accumulations of our modern chemical life-styles. Liquid detergents, bleach, shampoo, toilet deodorants, and a host of other chemicals such as paint cleaners and sludge removers. These are all toxic to the septic bacteria. They die and the sludge is not broken down, resulting in a fast buildup, clogged drains, and sewage back up.

The answer is a small separate tank for the sinks. It can be built adjacent to the main tank and then fed into the disposal field. The main tank then operates much more efficiently. To break down any grease in the smaller tank, a liquid bacteria can be added from time to time.

Of course, as mentioned in Chapter 1, you could consider the composting toilet. There are many new types on the market that can be installed inside your house and take up very little space. The only impediments to doing so may be legal ones. In some areas, composting toilets are not seen as a valid system by the health department despite the fact that they are odorless, do not cause a buildup of toxic waste, do not discharge liquid waste over large areas of ground and create a safe fertilizer at the same time. Outdoor composting toilets are an older idea and many people kept a pile of earth, a pile of leaves, and a pile of sawdust and ashes on hand to throw down the hole every other day. Each autumn the resulting compost was spread over the flowers or hayfield. North Americans generally have an aversion to using this compost on the vegetable garden, but the Chinese and Germans, for example, have done so for centuries.

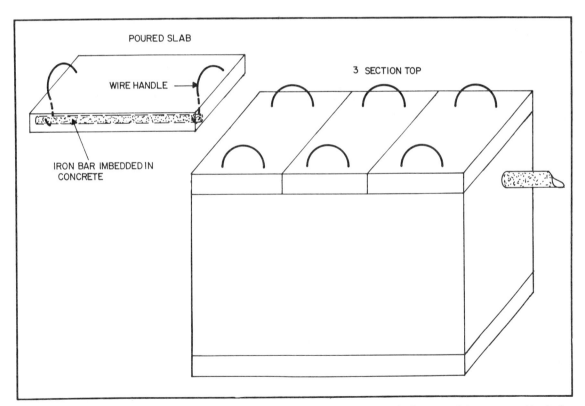

Fig. 7-9. If the tank is large, the top may be made in three sections for easy handling. Concrete slabs are poured in shallow (3-inch) forms with rebar imbedded for strength. Around the rebar, strong wire is wraped to form a handle when the concrete hardens. A slab 3″ × 3′ × 4′ weighs 400 to 500 pounds.

PUMPS

Unless your water is provided by city or town, you will need a pump to draw the well water into the house. Pumps used today generally fall into two categories: *piston pumps* and *jet pumps*. Both are powered by electric motors and draw water but there the similarity ends.

The piston pump is the type used extensively in older homes to draw water from dug wells and springs. It sits in the basement, usually on top of a large tank, and the motor turns a large wheel that drives the piston in the pump back and forth. This draws the water from the well by creating a sucking action on the intake pipe. The pump sounds similar to a make-and-break motor in a small fishing boat.

These pumps are extremely durable, require little maintenance, and are easily installed. They will draw water horizontally for a long distance but are limited to an average of 25 feet vertical draw. Thus, they are excellent for wells or springs that are no deeper than 25 feet. The distance from the house can be up to 100 feet or more. They usually require ¼-horsepower motors (Fig. 7-10).

Jet pumps work using an *impeller* instead of a piston. This is a wheel that spins inside the pump and draws water by means of centrifugal force. These pumps are more efficient than the piston types and are replacing them in contemporary homes. They have fewer moving parts and generally cost less than a piston pump of equal capacity.

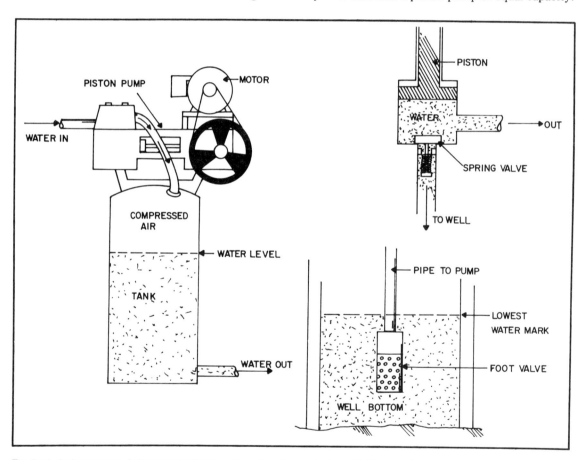

Fig. 7-10. A piston pump. A down stroke forces water out and an upstroke refills the chamber by drawing well water in through the spring valve. This water is stored in a tank where compressed air forces it through pipes and out the taps. A foot valve is installed in the well to prevent the water in the line to the pump from flowing back into the well.

They are divided into two types: shallow well and deep well pumps. The shallow well pump will draw water efficiently only to a depth of 25 feet, the same as a piston pump, which is sufficient for a dug well or spring. Where a drilled well is involved, the depth can vary from 35 to as much as several hundred feet. The shallow well jet pump is then converted to a deep well pump merely by the addition of a second line into the well. The jet section on the pump is introduced into the well for deep well use, whereas it remains attached to the pump for shallow well application.

Only one line is needed to draw water by suction from any well to a depth of 25 feet. Beyond 25 feet, it is much more efficient to push the water up and out of the well. This is what a deep well jet pump does. A deep well jet pump employs two lines, with the jet ejector placed in the well. The line that draws water from the well is equipped with a device called a *foot valve*. This valve is fastened to the end of the pipe nearest the well bottom and below the low water mark. (The low water mark is the lowest depth of the well at any time, either due to pumping or a dry spell.) The foot valve will admit water that is flowing into the pipe but prevents water from flowing back through the line into the well. Thus the pipe to the pump is continually full of water, which is necessary for the pump to work properly. Should the foot valve malfunction and permit the water to return to the well, then the pump, upon starting, will only suck air and will not draw water. This is termed *losing its prime*. To remedy this, the foot valve must be replaced and the pump filled with water by hand before restarting it. This is *priming the pump* and will reactivate the system.

A submersible deep well pump also is available. It is a long cylindrical pump that is completely submerged within the well and acts by pushing the water up the pipe. These pumps are usually more expensive but have two advantages over the other types. Since they are located in the well they are completely silent and they are the most efficient pumps to use for deep well demands. Maintenance is nil and I have heard of one of these pumps serving several families continuously for 17 years without a problem (Fig. 7-11).

Pumps are used to draw the well water but, to prevent the pump from running every time a tap is turned on, a storage tank is coupled to the pump. The water is forced into the tank under pressure, which in turn forces the water out of the tank and through the taps when they are turned on. Tanks are available in different sizes and types. The old type was simply a metal tank that was designed to be airtight. As the pump forced water into the tank, the air inside was compressed until a certain pressure was reached, approximately 45 psi. By turning on a tap, the compressed air pushed the water from the tank and through the line. These tanks had one disadvantage. If there was an air leak anywhere in the system, even a tiny one, the air pressure in the tank became difficult to maintain, with the result that the pump would eventually fill the tank with greater amounts of water. Thus, when the tap was turned on there was very little pressure to push the water out, consequently, the pump would come on every time the tap was opened. This is called *water-logging* the tank.

To overcome this problem, a new type of tank is available that has a rubber diaphragm built into the tank. Thus, air is pumped into the tank through a valve like that on a tire. The pressure is approximately 20 to 30 psi. When water enters this type of tank, it presses against the diaphragm to create back-pressure, and it cannot invade the space above the diaphragm. Water-logging is thereby prevented because the only exit the air pressure has is via the valve stem. Leaks in the system don't affect the tank pressure (See Fig. 7-11).

As with all systems there are advantages and disadvantages. For more specific information about each type of pump and its specifications, a salesman will only be too happy to oblige. For practical information, ask a friendly plumber or the owners of each type of pump before you decide what you need.

HEATING

Traditional methods of home heating include forced air, radiators (hot water), wood, coal, and solar. *Forced air* heating consists of a furnace and a fan, or *blower*. The heat from the furnace is blown throughout the house via *ductwork*—large metal tubes that

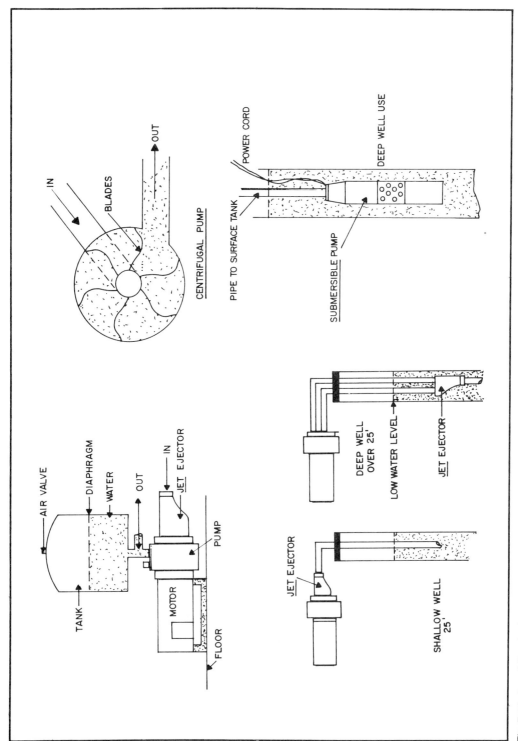

Fig. 7-11. A centrifugal or jet pump uses a spinning wheel, called an *impellor*, to draw water. As the wheel spins, it forces water out one pipe. Water is replaced via a hole at the center of the chamber. These pumps are very efficient and can be used for well depths in excess of 25 feet, which is the maximum depth for a piston pump. A submersible pump is used in a deep well. It pushes the water to the surface. These pumps are very durable and have the advantage of silent operation since they are located near the bottom of the well.

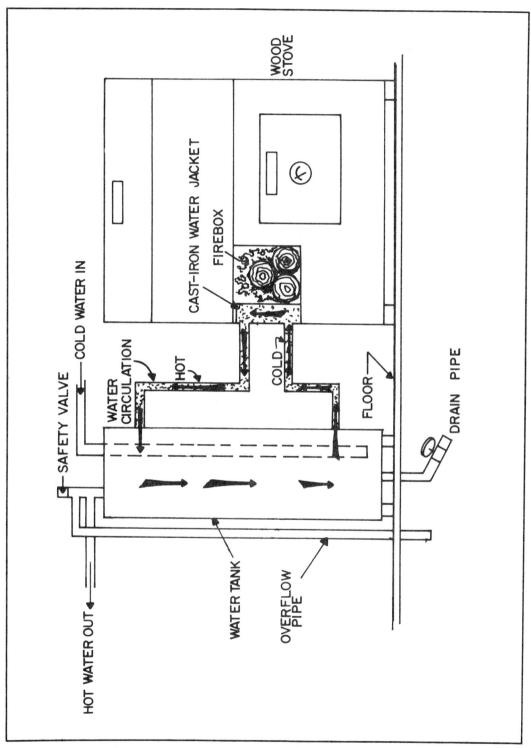

Fig. 7-12. Heating hot water with a woodstove. Water from the tank, circulates by convection through a cast iron chamber located in the firebox of the stove. The hot water is stored at the top of the tank and is forced out by the pressure in the cold water system.

run from the furnace to each room. A thermostat is set for the required temperature and controls the furnace by shutting the flame on and off. The typical forced air furnace burns oil or gas.

Radiator heating consists of a central furnace that heats a large tank of water. The water circulates throughout the house via pipes and in each room it passed through a radiator. These radiators present a large surface of piping to the air and as a result the heat from the water is transferred to the air in the room. The cooled water returns to the furnace for reheating. With this system, the domestic hot water is simply tapped off and not separately heated as is done with forced air.

Wood and coal heat traditionally provided warming fires in stoves, furnaces, and fireplaces. The heat radiated from one spot, and many of us remember the big central grill over the furnace where we stood to get warm in the mornings.

Solar heating, until recent years, was traditional only in warm climates. Modern technology has provided the means whereby solar heating is now a practical alternative for warming your house. All of these heat sources are currently being re-examined in the light of modern methods and the results are intriguing. For example, there is the forced air, thermostatically controlled, wood and coal furnace; the solar powered radiator/hot water system; and other combinations of the old and the new.

With non-renewable fossil fuels becoming increasingly high priced, the current trend is to develop the renewable resources such as wood and solar. These can very easily be incorporated into your house as a back-up system or as a supplementary heating unit. The method you choose will depend upon your locale, income, life-style, and creativity. Whatever system you opt for, there are possibilities available today that extend your choices well beyond those of the last half century.

You can utilize solar energy by having large south facing windows that will supply ample interior heat during sunny winter afternoons. There are some who have built large greenhouses directly adjoining their house. Here they grow fresh vegetables throughout the winter, use the captured heat to partially heat their house, and enjoy a green solarium at the same time.

Both solar and wood can be used to heat hot water. All of our hot water is provided by our wood cook stove as shown in Fig. 7-12. Cold water circulates through a cast iron chamber in the firebox of the stove and the emerging hot water is stored in the top of a large water tank. This system can also be connected to an oil or propane furnace with a few modifications, depending upon the type of structure of your furnace.

Solar water heating is achieved by use of a piping system to circulate water to a solar panel either located on the roof or a south facing wall. The sun's rays heat the water, which is stored in tanks in the house. The circulation is achieved with the use of a pump that causes the water to flow throughout the system continually while the sun shines. There are so many methods and systems that a detailed description would require a book, of which there are many excellent ones already in print.

Each heating system has its advantages and disadvantages. Fossil fuel systems obviously will require expensive fuel that will not get any cheaper in the future. The merits and drawbacks of wood heat are discussed more thoroughly in Chapter 9. Solar heat is the one that holds the most promise. Radiation from the sun is both renewable and constantly available. Despite cloudy days, new methodology is being developed that will store solar heat very efficiently. Combined with heat conservation techniques, the wasteful practices of the last century will become obsolete. Hopefully the emerging awareness of the need for greater respect for our environment will predominate in the choices made for the future.

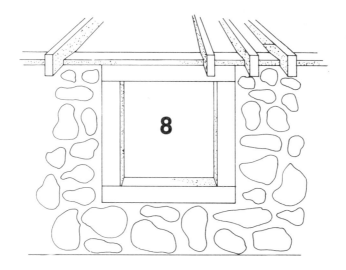

Wiring

WHERE WE LIVE, THE WIRING OF A HOUSE must be done by a licensed electrician. An owner/builder is prohibited, by law, from installing the electrical wiring. In other areas of the country the local bylaws are different: it is legal to do your own wiring, but it must be inspected by a licensed official before it is deemed serviceable. It is up to you to ascertain the local requirements governing house wiring for your area.

Sources of information covering bylaws and wiring codes are available at government offices and sometimes libraries. We received excellent advice and money saving ideas by talking to local electricians whom we picked out of the phone book. Before finally deciding on one electrician for the job, we talked to several and asked for their price quotes. We also asked local building suppliers for recommendations and talked to people who had work done by various electricians. This proved to be well worth the effort. The price quotes varied widely as did the quality of workmanship. We hired a man who worked fast and efficiently and whose price was reasonble.

Another source we contacted was an instructor of electrical wiring at a vocational school. His friendly advice was very valuable and he knew of current revisions in local bylaws that were not as yet listed in the code book on house wiring.

Therefore, to have some knowledge of the basics of wiring is a must for these reasons. It enables you to talk intelligently to the electrician concerning your needs and requirements, and it gives you an understanding of the function of such items as entrance boxes, meter bases, switch boxes and outlets, types of wire, etc. You can then include in your planning the necessary prerequisites for wiring and will be aware of what you can and cannot do regarding your ideas for electrical service throughout your house.

DETERMINING YOUR NEEDS

Providing electrical power for your house will depend upon several factors: your current lifestyle, future plans, bylaws, and new alternate energy sources. Regarding life-style, do you have electrical tools, or plan to? Will you use electrical appliances such as clothes washer and dryer, kitchen range, stereo, and so on? How about electric heat or hot water? Each of these items requires electricity in different amounts and will have to be included in your design plans. Do you have future plans that will require additional sources of electricity? Perhaps an outside workshop, garage, a pump for the fountain in the garden pool you promised yourself? These will require advance planning.

The local bylaws concerning house wiring will detail the steps you must take in servicing your house. The layout of each light switch is determined within certain limits, as are all the other facets of wiring. For example, it is usually not permissible to have an outlet near any water source such as a sink or tub. The number of outlets for each room is specified plus the size of the wiring to be used. In some areas it is mandatory to provide a house with all the electrical service it could possibly need, now and in the future, the idea being that future owners will want all-electric living. Thus a balance must be reached. After determining your needs for now and later on, then you must examine the minimum requirements by law and see how they relate to each other. Usually the bylaws will provide for all the wiring requirements you need and more.

A consideration that is appearing more and more in the media and the minds of builders concerns souces of alternate energy. If you have chosen to live without electricity, then the foregoing concerns will not affect you, and you will no doubt benefit from the substantial savings gained by avoiding the plenitude of electrical gadgets. But if you want electrical service, even in small amounts, then some source of supply will be necessary.

The current intensive investigation and experimentation into wind and water power as sources of electricity has placed them in a position where they are becoming financially feasible for the owner/builder. There is a wealth of information available on the subject of small windmills and home hydro-power projects. If this is a possibility for you, then it is very easy to obtain detailed information and even sources of materials that did not exist a few years ago. All that is necessary to get started is a trip to the library or your local magazine rack. Still, the basic goal is to produce electricity, which was once considered a magic fluid that flowed through a wire.

MEASURING ELECTRICITY

Basically, no one knows what electricity is. That it has force and involves motion is undeniable, especially to anyone who has ever stuck their finger in a light socket. This history of the discovery and evolution of electricity is fascinating and makes interesting reading particularly when one recognizes it as the force that shapes our civilization, nuclear power nonwithstanding. The ancient Egyptians were intrigued with the effects of rubbing the fur of a cat to produce static electricity: that same force has since evolved into the complex guidance systems of computer controlled spacecraft.

Electricity is easily understood by using the analogy of water in a pipe. The pipe represents a wire and the water the electricity. The amount of water in the pipe is equivalent to the amount of electricity, measured in *amperes*, and called *current*. The force with which the electricity flows is measured in *volts* and called *voltage*. The resistance or obstruction that the wire gives to the electrical flow is measured in *ohms* and is called its *resistance*. Expressed in a formula, the relation of one to another is:

$$I = E/R \text{ where } I = \text{Amperage}, E = \text{Voltage}, R = \text{Resistance}$$

This formula is *Ohm's law* and is the cornerstone of electrical mathematics (Fig. 8-1).

This knowledge is basic if you wish to understand how you are charged for your use of electricity by the utility company and how you can reduce your power bills. Electricity enters your house and runs your appliances. The amount of electricity each appliance uses is measured in *watts* and is called power. The total amount of power used by all your appliances and heating devices is measured by the meter that usually is installed outside of the house. This is the power meter, and it measures the total amount of power you use in kilowatt hours.

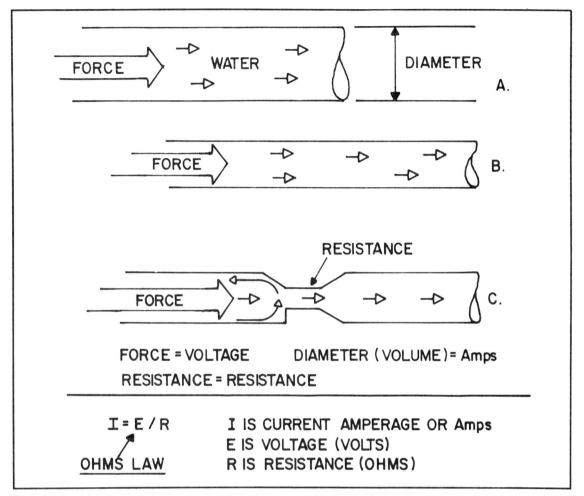

FORCE = VOLTAGE   DIAMETER (VOLUME)= Amps

RESISTANCE = RESISTANCE

$$I = E / R$$

OHMS LAW

I IS CURRENT AMPERAGE OR Amps

E IS VOLTAGE (VOLTS)

R IS RESISTANCE (OHMS)

Fig. 8-1. Electricity is analogous to water in a pipe. The volume of water equals current or amperage, the force of water is voltage, and the resistance of the pipe to water flow is its ohmage. Expressed in a formula $I = E/R$ (Ohm's law).

If a toaster requires 1000 watts of power to operate, it uses 1 *kilowatt*. If it ran for one hour it would use 1 *kilowatt/hour* of power. You pay for each kilowatt/hour of electricity you use (Fig. 8-2).

By knowing the power required by each of your appliances, you can calculate the amount of electricity you will be using and its cost. The price of each kilowatt/hour is available from the power company. It is important to learn these facts and discover just how much power is unnecessary and wasted in our homes.

SERVICE ENTRANCE

Electricity is generated by various means, using fossil fuels and water power primarily, and delivered to your door via transmission lines attached to wooden poles. The voltages (analogous to pressure) generated initially are very high in order to facilitate transmission over long distances but are reduced down via *transformers* (those garbage cans atop the poles) before entering your house.

Almost all electrical devices in use in the United States and Canada require either 240 volts of electricity or 120 volts in order to operate. (This

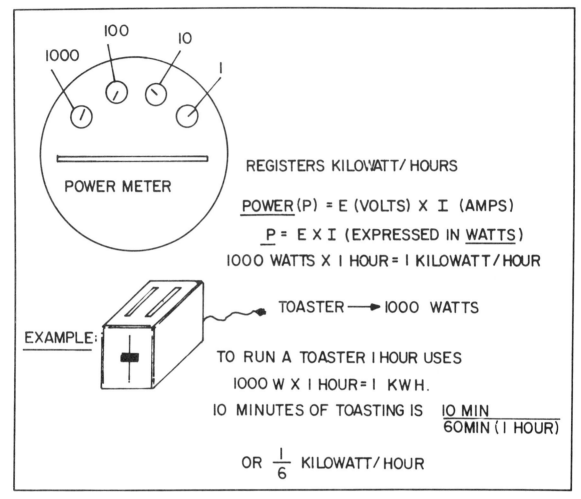

REGISTERS KILOWATT / HOURS

POWER (P) = E (VOLTS) X I (AMPS)

P = E X I (EXPRESSED IN WATTS)

1000 WATTS X 1 HOUR = 1 KILOWATT / HOUR

TOASTER ⟶ 1000 WATTS

EXAMPLE:

TO RUN A TOASTER 1 HOUR USES

1000 W X 1 HOUR = 1 KWH.

10 MINUTES OF TOASTING IS $\dfrac{10\ MIN}{60\ MIN\ (1\ HOUR)}$

OR $\dfrac{1}{6}$ KILOWATT / HOUR

Fig. 8-2. The amount of power used by a household is measured using a power meter which expresses power in terms of kilowatt hours. A kilowatt is 1000 watts of power. Power = E (volts × I (amps). Using 1000 watts for 1 hour equals 1 kilowatt hour.

doesn't apply to battery operated transistor devices, of course. Some of these do, however, have an attachment to make the device run from household current.) The voltage requirements of each device is stated directly on the appliance. Most requirements are for 120 volts. (Stereo, washer, small appliances, tools, lights, pumps, etc.) 240 volts is used wherever great heat production is required (electric heaters, kitchen range, clothes dryer, welding machines, water heaters, etc.).

When houses were first served with electricity, in many instances they were wired only for 120 volts. This was because there were not many heavy electrical appliances and demand was only for lights and pumps. Many old houses were still wired for only 120 volts. Nowadays, almost all houses are wired for both 120 and 240 volts, leaving no choice for the builder when installing electric power.

The wiring system runs from the power pole in three wires to your house. Two of them are *live* or *hot* and one *neutral* or *ground*. Between the two hot wires is measured 240 volts and from one hot to neutral is measured 120 volts.

These wires pass through a meter before entering your house so that the amount of electricity you use can be recorded by the power company. The meter is usually on the outside of the house but in some older houses it is on the inside. (Plan to have it installed on the outside of your house to make it convenient for the power company to read it. It should be situated at eye level near the spot where the power lines will enter.)

In order to fasten this meter to a stone house, it is necessary to anchor an oak board (oak being long lasting and weather resistant) to the wall using bolts imbedded in the pointing mortar. The meter is attached to the board along with part of the galvanized metal conduit that protects the wires from the weather and any accident. The conduit then projects through the hole you remembered to build into the wall. Ours is a 2½-inch hole (Fig. 8-3).

Once through the wall, the wires pass into a metal box called a *service entrance* where the main on/off switch is located. The electricity is then passed through fuses and divided up to be distributed throughout the house (Fig. 8-4).

Out of the service entrance box come heavy wires carrying 240 volts for your appliances that require it and lighter wires carrying 120 volts for lights and so on. The location of the box is often determined by the electrical codes and you must make your plans accordingly, prior to any construction. For example, an entrance box must not be located in a hard-to-reach place or near any water outlets.

Service entrances are rated in terms of amperage. They are capable of handling varying amounts of amperage depending upon the amount of power (wattage) you will need. The usual service entrance boxes are 60 or 100 amps rated. You can determine your requirements beforehand by adding up all the energy your appliances and other devices will use. Very often the rating of the service entrance is pre-determined by law but if you have a choice then this knowledge will assist you in making a decision.

DISTRIBUTION

The distribution of electricity throughout your house is accomplished using various types of wire. This, again, is determined by the bylaws but basically a lighter wire containing two conductors and a ground is used for the wall outlets, and a heavier three wire and ground is used for the kitchen range, heaters, dryers, and so on. These wires are installed in the walls and fastened in place using special wire staples.

All wire connections must be made in metal junction boxes, and all switches and outlets must be grounded (Fig. 8-5). These are basic safety measures. Just as the fuses are there for protection from fire and overloading, so the ground connections and junction boxes are for personal safety. For example, if you were operating a power tool such as an electric drill and a short circuit developed in the wiring of the drill, the resulting electrical surge would be directed through the house wiring instead of your body. A fuse would blow and shut the system down.

There are many types of wire: waterproof plastic coated wire, metal encased wire (*armored-flexible cable*), and so on. Find out which is the required type so that you don't unnecessarily install an expensive wire that is not needed. By knowing exactly what you require, you can buy the materials in advance, as we did, thereby taking advantage of any sales. Electrical parts, as well as wire, can often be obtained at savings by scouting for leftover materials from other construction projects. Electricians often have leftover materials they will sell below retail prices. Become knowledgeable about the wiring and if you have to hire an electrician, perhaps he will be happy to let you assist him, thereby saving both time and money.

The wiring of the house is done during the framing stage and is called the *rough wiring*. Finish wiring is the installation of light fixtures, cover plates, stoves, etc. In order to install the wiring, the location of such items as electric range, washer, dryer, refrigerator, freezer, and so on must be known. Wiring is installed between the walls, under the floor, and above the ceiling (unless it is an open cathedral-type). Different methods are legal in one area and not in others. Basically, all wire must be supported by either stapling it to beams or studs or by drilling holes through the studs and feeding the wire through.

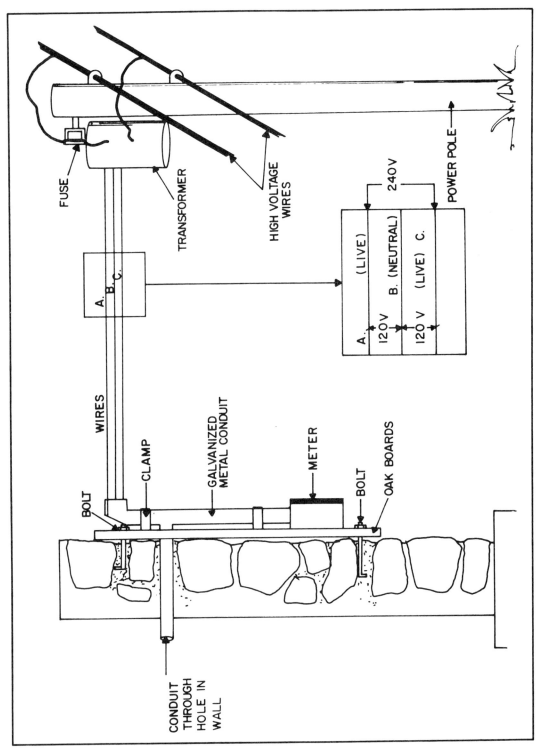

Fig. 8-3. Electricity is fed from the power lines into your house via a power meter and metal conduit. To attach this meter and conduit to a stone house, a hole must be built into the wall about 2½ inches in diameter. Conduit is attached to a board bolted to the wall. The bolts are imbedded in the mortar while it is wet.

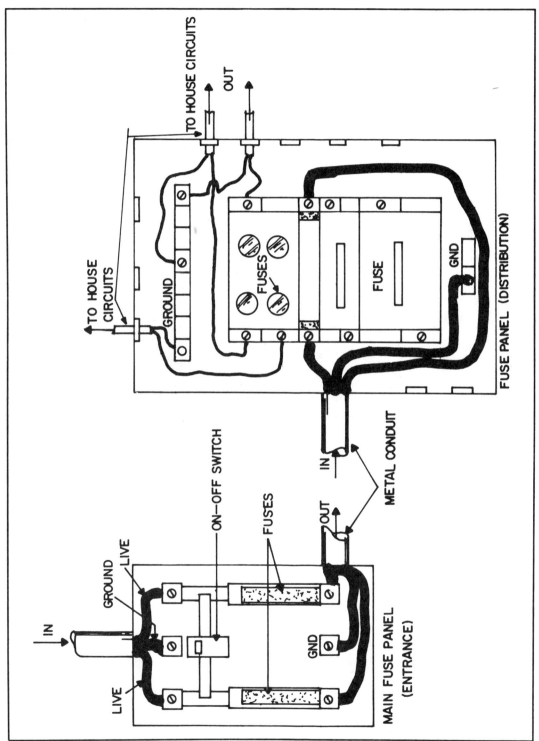

Fig. 8-4. When the electric wires enter the house, they are connected to a large switch and two fuses. They are distributed through various other fuses to the house circuits in each room. This distribution panel is the service entrance. It is rated in terms of amperage—60 or 100 amps is standard.

137

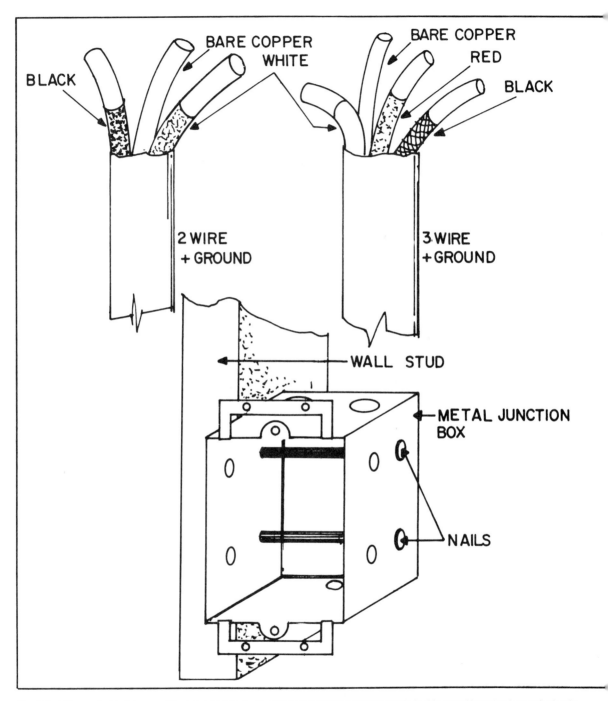

Fig. 8-5. All household wiring must be insulated and grounded with all connections made inside metal junction boxes for basic safety. Wire types vary and depend upon the voltage and amperage used, plus household location. (i.e., between walls, underground, etc.) Generally two wires and ground are used for 120 volt service and three wires and ground for 240 volt. The thickness of the wire depends upon the amount of amperage it carries.

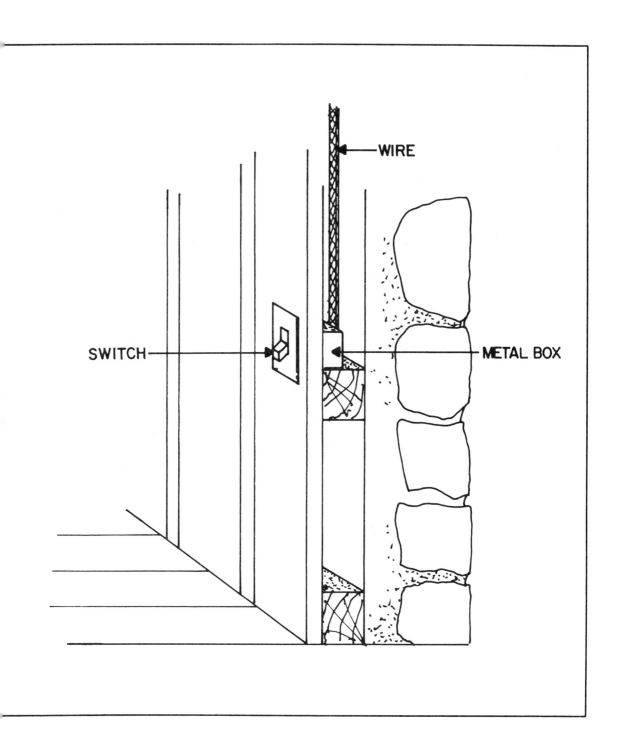

WIRE

SWITCH

METAL BOX

Each wire that emerges from the fuse panel will be connected to a number of outlets—one *circuit*. Because each fuse is rated for a certain amperage (i.e., 15 amps), then the circuit attached to it cannot exceed a maximum of 15 amps without blowing the fuse. In older houses, the fuse panel held four or six fuses for the whole house. This was sufficient because there was low power demand being made. Today, fuse panels may contain upward of 16 to 20 fuses for 120-volt circuits plus separate fuses for the 240-volt circuits.

If you will be requiring any heavy-duty outlets such as for welding gear or a kiln for pottery, then other separate circuits will be necessary. If you are permitted to do the wiring yourself, subject to inspection before hookup, then a more thorough knowledge of wiring will be in order. The knowledge required to wire a house is not complicated, but you will have to adhere to the specified codes laid down for safety reasons. Once the wiring is complete and in use there is very little that can go wrong. There are no moving parts aside from light switches, which occasionally wear out. When charging a light switch or doing any electrical repair, do so with the main switch off. Believe it or not, there are still those who think that standing on one leg or holding an arm behind their back will make it possible to get a severe shock. I advise you not to put it to the test.

Never replace a fuse with one rated at a higher amperage and definitely never use a penny or tin foil to replace a blown fuse. Find out why the fuse blew in the first place and correct the malfunction. Fuses are there to prevent fire due to overheated wires. Wires will overheat if they are forced to carry excessive electrical current either by a short circuit or by overloading a circuit.

Short circuits are caused when a live wire is connected directly to ground. There is no resistance to current flow and as a result the amperage increases instantly, causing heating and very often sparking. Old buildings often burned down because rats had chewed the insulation off the wires and caused them to short circuit. If the fuses were too large, or pennies used, the sparking continued until adjacent wood caught fire.

Overloading occurs when too great a demand is placed on a circuit by plugging in too many electrical devices simultaneously. That is why the use of multiple plug-in devices is not recommended. The excessive number of electric items will draw a large current and result in overheating and finally a fire. If your house burned to the ground due to an electrical fire and it was discovered that a penny or tin foil was in the fuse box, the insurance would be null and void, if you were alive to try and collect. Electrical fires, causing extensive damage and loss of life, can be so easily avoided that it is amazing so many still occur. Using frayed extension cords, leaving an iron on, using too large a fuse, etc., are among the reasons we hear for electrically caused fires.

ALTERNATE POWER SOURCES

It is becoming easier for an individual to produce all, or part of, his own electrical power. Once again, this is due to advances in technology and the rising price of buying electricity, which is making home systems more and more competitive.

Before you can consider the ways and means of generating electricity, you need a source of motive power other than fossil fuels. These are water, wind, and sun. If you live near a stream or brook, you have potential hydro-power. In an area exposed to wind, there exists potential windmill power. In sunny climates, solar power is available. Wind and water power are a mechanical means of generating power involving moving parts; solar power is static and molecular. Solar power used to generate electricity is presently quite expensive for an individual undertaking. The photoelectric cells needed to convert sunlight to electricity are not manufactured cheaply enough as yet to warrant the system for home use by the average family. Technology is advancing so rapidly, however, that there may already be systems available of which I am unaware.

The water and wind systems have been developed enough to present a feasible alternative to commercial power. There are presently systems offered for sale by companies that specialize in wind and water power. Depending upon the amount of power you wish to generate, they have the equipment available in a range of prices. There are also

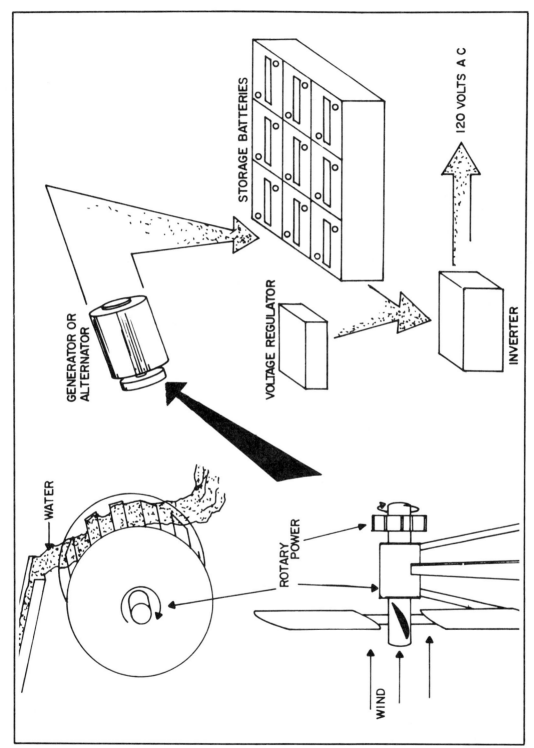

WATER

STORAGE BATTERIES

GENERATOR OR ALTERNATOR

VOLTAGE REGULATOR

120 VOLTS A C

INVERTER

ROTARY POWER

WIND

Fig. 8-6. Alternate energy sources include water and wind power. Water wheels and windmills use natural forces to create rotary motion to drive a device that produces electricity. The electrical power is stored in bank of batteries for use in times of low wind or water power. A voltage regulator controls the flow of electricity to the batteries and an inverter converts dc voltage to ac for household use.

those who make their own systems from scratch.

Each system needs motive power to generate the electricity, a means of storing it and devices to smooth out any fluctuations in the supply and convert it from dc to ac for household use.

To harness the motive power of a small stream, there are several methods from which to choose. The simplest, and oldest, method is a *water wheel*, a small version of the huge wheels that used to power sawmills and gristmills not so long ago. The wheel is placed in a position where water can be directed to fall on the top of it and cause it to revolve. (Modern methods use turbines that are placed in the current of the stream. The flow of water through the turbine's blades cause its internal rotor to spin.) It does not take a very large stream to turn a small water wheel but make sure that the stream doesn't go dry in summer.

For wind power, the average wind strength for your area must be ascertained. Ask the local weather office. Even if the average wind speed is low (3 to 5 miles per hour) it can still be harnessed with a windmill. The only other feature to be looked at is the topography of your land. Are you surrounded by trees or hills and would a windmill on a tower be exposed to sufficient wind to turn the blades? On the other hand, if your area is exposed to a lot of wind, such as on a hill by the seacoast, a windmill is even more feasible. There are methods of controlling the windmill so that high winds don't damage it. A windmill has a mechanism that orients the blades towards the wind, but if the wind becomes too strong, the blades must be reoriented to prevent damage. At one time this was done manually, but there are new designs that change the pitch of the blades automatically. This allows the windmill to rotate slowly, even in a gale force wind.

Electricity is produced by connecting the rotary action of the water wheel or windmill to an electrical generator or alternator. These devices produce electricity by electromagnetic means. Large ones are used by the power companies and smaller ones are found in automobiles, planes, ships, and so on, wherever there is a need to produce electricity. The electricity generated by them varies in type and amount depending upon design and use. They can produce alternating current or direct current, in different voltages and amperages. For household use, alternating current is required, the standard is 60 cycles per second (60 *hertz*) at 120 volts or 240 volts. Direct current is the type used in automobiles and provided by a standard 12-volt battery.

The output of a system connected to a waterwheel is fairly steady because of continual water flow, but heavy rain or a dry spell will alter the force of the stream. Likewise for a windmill. While the wind blows and the blades are turning, there is electrical output but when they are still there is nothing generated. The means to control these fluctuations is a group of storage batteries connected together. Several batteries are needed to store the amount of electricity that may be required during periods of low output. The output from the batteries is direct current (dc) usually 12- or 24-volt. To use this in your house it must be changed to 120 volts ac using a device called an *inverter*. A dam system is used to control the amount of water fed to the water wheel and can boost the flow in a low period and reduce flow in a flood (Fig. 8-6).

There is an abundant source of detailed information available on the subject of alternative energy sources. There are retail suppliers for those who wish to buy outright. For those who want to do-it-themselves, there are many books and magazines that offer all sorts of ways and means to construct a system to suit your local and particular needs.

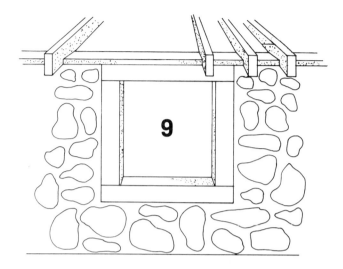

Porch, Fireplace, and Chimney

As mentioned in the introduction, we planned to build our house in three stages. the main house, complete with bathroom, bedroom, kitchen/living room; then a stone porch; and finally a third section comprising a spare bedroom and an all-purpose room. (Barbara's surprise room.) Each section would be constructed in one summer for three consecutive years, thereby giving us plenty of building time plus spare time for other pursuits.. We would be able to pay as we go so that, when completed, our house would be mortgage-free.

The porch was built in one summer using the methods employed for the main house. The footing was poured first, then the walls of stone and concrete were erected. The window frames were built of 6 × 6-inch beams. The only differences in the basic method were in the means of joining the two sections together. From the floor plan of Fig. 1-9, it can be seen where the porch was located with reference to the main house.

To join the porch walls to the main house a 6 × 6-inch beam was installed in the house walls while they were being built. This beam was placed where

the juncture of the walls was to be. Large spikes were driven into this beam and the porch walls were poured directly against the beam. When hardened, the porch walls gripped the spikes and were firmly anchored in place. The seams between the porch and main walls were filled with mortar when the pointing was done (Fig. 9-1).

PORCH CONSTRUCTION

To begin, we dug a footing trench. It began at the main house next to the 6 × 6 beam, ran 10 feet west, then 8 feet north, and back 10 feet east to end at the other 6 × 6 junction beam. The footing, like the house footing, was poured 20 inches wide and varied in depth due to bedrock. Where it sat on bedrock it was 1 foot thick but elsewhere it was built below the frost line up to a thickness of 3 feet.

We set our forms on the completed footing and maintained the wall thickness of 10 inches. We then built the walls using the slipform technique. We installed two window frames in the porch walls but, unlike the frames in the house, they reached to the plate and formed part of it. Refer to Fig. 3-18. The

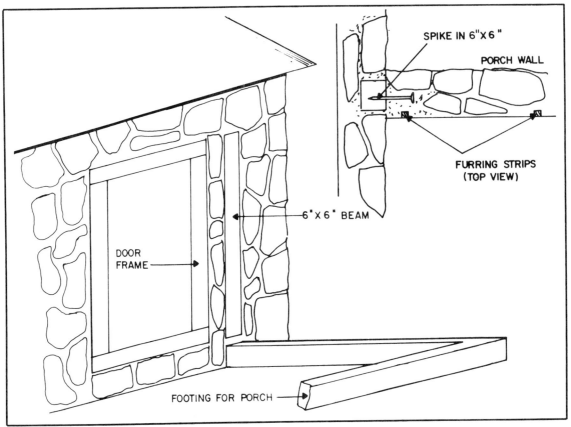

Fig. 9-1. The walls for a stone porch are attached using an imbedded 6 × 6 beam as an anchoring point. Heavy spikes are driven into the beam and the porch walls poured against them. When hard, the concrete grips these spikes and holds the walls firmly together. The seams are then pointed with mortar.

frames were made of 6 × 6-inch pine and were 4 × 4 feet and 3½ × 5 feet in size. We also installed a door in the south wall of the porch. Since the porch had only three walls, two windows, and a door, it was built very quickly. When the walls were completed, we pointed them, after first chipping off any flakes of loose concrete and snipping the protruding wires.

Into the base of the walls went vents to keep the floor from becoming damp in summer. These vents were made in the same way as the vents for the main house and opened under the floor.

The porch roof was designed as a simple shed roof and was to become part of the slope of the main roof. The pitch for the roof was low, about 1½":1'.

(This pitch we subsequently discovered to be a bit too shallow. Although the rain water runs off easily, the snow in the winter does not and if there is a lot of snow it is necessary to clear the roof with a shovel. Otherwise, the snow melts on the bottom due to the warmth from the house and creates a buildup of ice that gradually grows thicker. A steeper pitch is better if you live in an area of heavy snow.)

The slope for the wall tops was achieved as follows: As the walls reached their planned height they were leveled using the methods outlined in Chapter 3. A 2 × 8-inch plate was placed on top of the west wall parallel to the main house. A 2 × 6-inch box header was nailed to the ends of the house rafters and the porch rafters were nailed from the header to the plate. The rafters sloped above the level wall top, perpendicular to the house, outlining the area of the porch wall that remained to be built. Forms were placed on either side of the wall top and enclosed the rafters. We then filled in underneath the rafters with stone and concrete to form the small triangular section that was left (Fig. 9-2).

The roof was boarded in with 1-inch lumber and covered with rolled felt. Galvanized metal was nailed directly to the roof. We did not strap the porch roof, as we did for the main house roof, since we were not going to insulate the porch roof on the outside. The roof boards were extended 1 foot on either side of the porch walls to allow wide eaves. The rafter ends also extended 1 foot beyond the wall to complete a 1-foot wide eave all around the porch.

The metal roofing was attached to the main roof by sliding it underneath the metal of the main roof about 1½ inches and on the other end by leaving a projection of 1½ inches beyond the rafter ends. To do this, the lower end to the metal roofing on the main roof had to be raised up by removing the nails. A silicone sealing compound was used to seal the joint between the main and porch roofs to prevent any leak due to heavy snow buildup. Then the main roof was renailed simultaneously with the porch roof (Fig. 9-3).

On the inside of the porch roof, insulating batts were stapled between the rafters and a vapor barrier added. The ceiling was finished by nailing planed lumber to the rafters. Vents were installed in the fascia board on the rafter ends so that fresh air could circulate above the insulation and vent any condensation to the outside (Fig. 9-4).

To make the porch floor, 2 × 6-inch floor joists were laid with their ends resting on the footing. Since the span was just 7 feet mid-supports were not needed. It was boarded over in the same fashion as the floor in the main house, using 1-inch lumber. The walls were finished in board and batten style, using furring strips to anchor the strapping and the vertical wall boards. There was no plumbing to be installed and the wiring was quite simple, requiring only one outlet and one light switch.

FIREPLACE

For some people a fireplace is a "must" on their list of priorities for their house. There is no denying the allure of a crackling fire in an attractive stone or brick fireplace. Unfortunately the allure is mostly visual because in a conventional fireplace up to 90 percent of the heat will go up the chimney and be lost. Very few old-type fireplaces are being built in contemporary homes because they do waste most of the heat, and they are quite difficult for a novice to build. Fireplaces, if improperly built, will not only waste heat but are often very smoky. The smoke will not draw up the chimney but instead seeps out the front of the fireplace causing smoke damage, smarting eyes, and considerable frustration. This problem is a bad one because it is due to improper design of the throat of the fireplace and thus not easily corrected. (Other causes of a smoky fireplace are discussed later.)

To circumvent this wasting of heat, many fireplace builders are incorporating steel liners in place of the brick firebox. These liners are bought ready-made in many shapes and sizes and sporting various features. Essentially they are a steel box designed for the efficient burning of wood. They reduce the incidence of smoky fireplaces and radiate the majority of heat into the house, sometimes using fans and vent systems. They are built into the fireplace and insulated from the surrounding stone or brickwork. When the fireplace is faced with layer of stone or brick, the appearance is like that of an old-fashioned fireplace.

Design

There are three common methods of building a fireplace and chimney, either using concrete blocks and bricks, stone, or a combination of these materials. Using concrete blocks and bricks makes the building of a fireplace faster than with stone alone since the bricks are laid atop one another quite easily. The freehand method of laying stone in a stiff mortar takes more time, but with patience and attention to detail satisfactory results can be obtained. Before tackling a stone fireplace or chim-

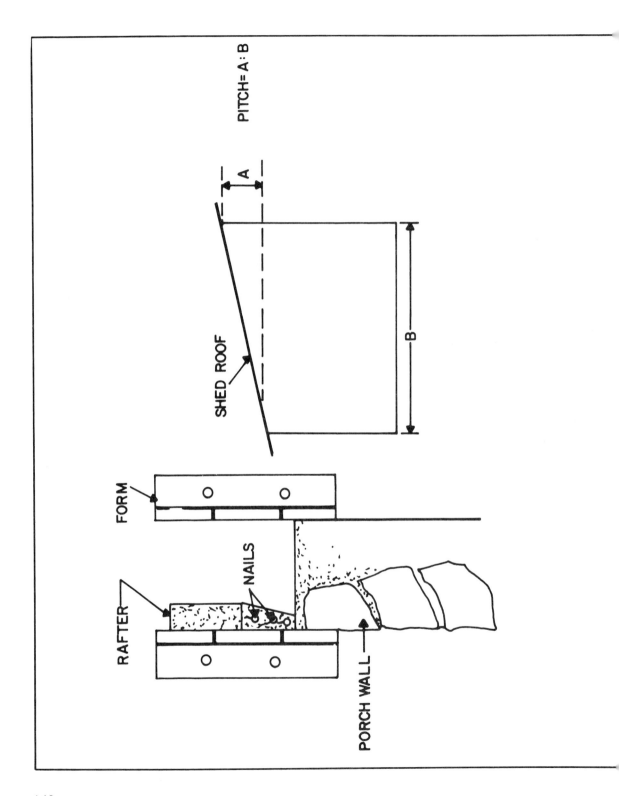

PITCH = A : B

A

B

SHED ROOF

FORM

NAILS

RAFTER

PORCH WALL

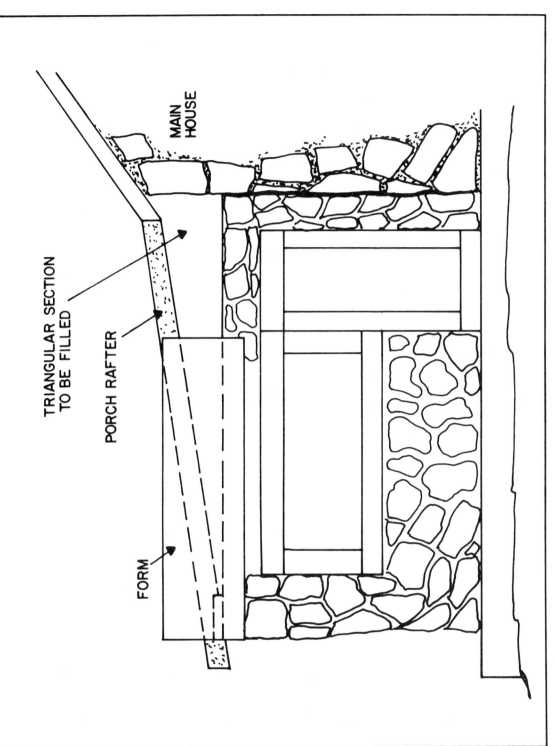

TRIANGULAR SECTION
TO BE FILLED

PORCH RAFTER

FORM

MAIN
HOUSE

Fig. 9-2. We used a shed roof on our porch and attached the rafters to the ends of the main house rafters. The triangular space under the porch rafters was filled with stone and concrete using the wooden forms.

147

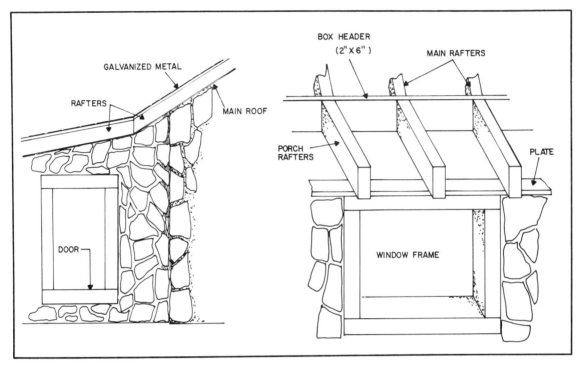

Fig. 9-3. A box header was nailed to the ends of the rafters of the main house. The porch rafters were attached to this box header and to the wall plate of the porch. The window frame in the porch reached to the plate, thereby eliminating any stonework above the window.

ney, some time spent getting the feel of freehand stonework is a definite asset. Building a stone barbeque or a garden wall will invest the basic skills that will be needed for a more demanding fireplace and chimney project.

Fireplace designs are legion but basically they consist of a *chamber* to burn the wood, a *throat* or *smoke shelf* to baffle downdrafts, and a *chimney* for the smoke to escape (Fig. 9-5). The firebox of the fireplace is lined with *firebrick* that will withstand extreme heat without cracking. At the back of the firebox is a tilted brick wall that forms the smoke shelf to baffle any downdrafts. These gusts of air rush down the chimney when the wind is blowing and can blow sparks into the house along with great plumes of smoke. The smoke shelf and the firebox must be built in the proper ratio to one another to work effectively.

At the top of the baffle is a movable metal plate called a *damper*. The damper serves two purposes:

it can be adjusted to regulate the burning of the fire in varying wind conditions (on very windy days it would be almost closed to limit draw up the flue. This results in a slow fire, saved wood, and retained heat). Second, the damper is used to completely close off the flue when the fire is out. This prevents downdrafts from blowing fine ash into the room and more importantly, prevents what heat there is in the house from being sucked up the chimney. (Here is a major disadvantage of a conventional fireplace. If you light a cozy fire in the winter, you have to leave the damper open to let the smoke escape, even when only glowing embers are left. Then, when you go to bed, the fire must be completely out or otherwise, while you sleep, the fireplace converts itself into a large vacuum cleaner and the heat in the house is very quickly sucked up the chimney when the fire dies out. With the steel liners there are features, such as removable doors, which can be used to close off the firebox when

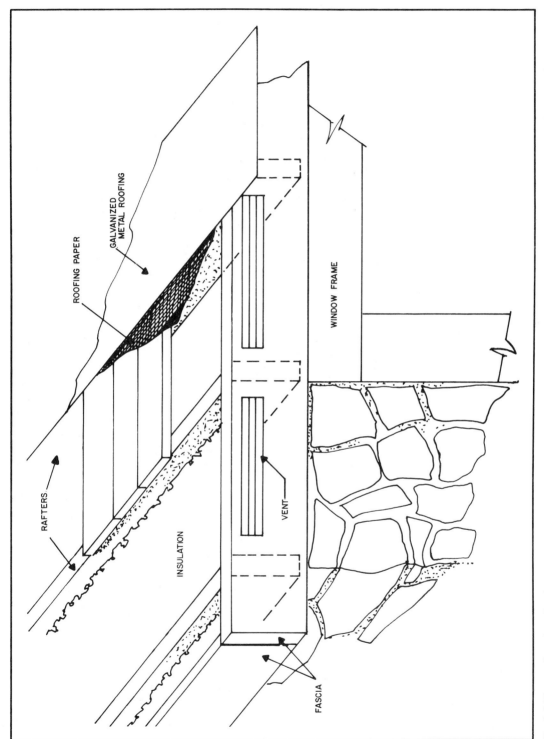

Fig. 9-4. The porch roof was insulated on the inside with fiberglass batts between the rafters. The roof was covered with boards, building paper, and galvanized metal. Vents in the fascia board remove condensation above the insulation.

149

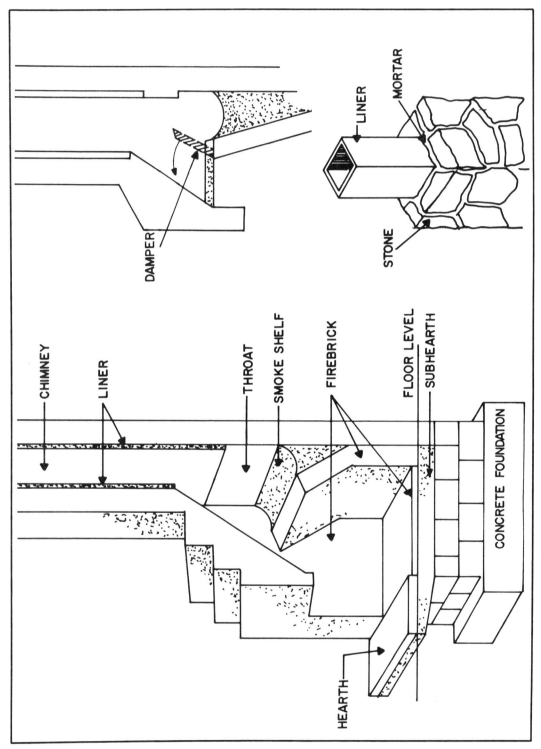

Fig. 9-5. A conventional fireplace consists of a firebrick firebox, a smoke shelf and throat, damper, and flue. The damper regulates the burning of the fire and closes off the flue when the fire is out. The flue is lined with clay to inhibit creosote buildup and serves as a heat shield for the surrounding stone or brickwork.

Labels in figure: DAMPER, MORTAR, LINER, STONE, CHIMNEY, LINER, THROAT, SMOKE SHELF, FIREBRICK, FLOOR LEVEL, SUBHEARTH, HEARTH, CONCRETE FOUNDATION

needed. Some have automatic draft controls that shut the draft when required.)

Inside the flue there is a liner made of fired clay. This protects the flue from cracking and also inhibits the buildup of creosote on the interior walls of the flue. It does not completely prevent creosote buildup, however, and any chimney will need periodic cleaning.

Construction

The construction of a fireplace and chimney requires much planning and involves considerable detail. To describe it fully would necessitate a book in itself, of which there are many. For stone houses, however, the essential technique for building a fireplace is basically the same.

A fireplace for a stone house must of necessity be an integral part of the walls if its design includes an outside chimney. Thus, during construction of the walls a gap of the required size is left into which the fireplace will later be added. The building sequence is then foundation, walls, fireplace, and roof. The house plans must take the fireplace into consideration from the beginning and proceed accordingly. It cannot be added later, as is often done for a frame house.

A chimney is easier to build since it is essentially a straight pipe to evacuate smoke and gases. (i.e., a chimney separate from a fireplace and meant for use with a woodstove, or oil or gas furnace.)

Both a fireplace and a chimney require a solid foundation placed well below the frost line. For a fireplace, a large reinforced concrete pad is poured to support the weight of the fireplace and chimney, which can easily range in the vicinity of 25 to 50 tons. The pad should extend at least a foot or more beyond the base of the fireplace in all directions.

If you choose to build an inside fireplace or chimney, then the pad is poured inside the house and the chimney will be freestanding. The reasons for building a fireplace/chimney completely inside the house are that it can be centrally located and, in an open style house, the heat is more evenly distributed; the heat from the warmed stones of the flue is added to the house and not wasted; the fireplace burns more efficiently since heat is not lost by having to battle the cooling effect of the outside air in winter; the stonework of the chimney is visible on the inside and adds to the overall aesthetics of the fireplace.

An inside fireplace is considered to be freestanding because it is not directly anchored to the floors or the roof. It must therefore be built with a solid base, be soundly reinforced, and as upright and plumb as possible. The floor is then built around the base of the fireplace and the roof built around the top.

After the footing is ready, a layer of concrete block, fastened in mortar, is built up to the required level and a layer of firebrick is put down. On top of this sits the steel liner, also fastened in a bed of mortar. Around the liner, the stonework is erected. Between the liner and the stonework, as it is built, is placed a layer of fiberglass insulation held in place by mortar. This serves as a buffer between the liner and the stone to protect the mortar from cracking due to the heat from the fire. It is also needed because the steel liner will expand when hot and contract while cooling, and the stonework has no "give" to it.

When the fireplace liner is completely encased, the stonework continues upward to form the flue. The flue is lined with clay tile as previously mentioned and a protruding ledge is formed inside the flue for the tile to sit on. The tile is also insulated from the stonework by a layer of mortar. Every effort must be made to keep the flue plumb as it continues skyward. With stonework, it is difficult to use a level but a string fastened to the rafters and weighted to hang down vertically will indicate the general outline of the corners of the chimney. Where the chimney exits the roof, flashing must be installed, and this is discussed after the following section (Fig. 9-6).

Stone Chimney

An outside stone chimney can be built without leaving a gap in the house walls. Instead, it is attached to the existing outside wall. Two-by-fours are installed vertically in the stone walls in the same fashion as furring strips, except that they are on the outside of the wall. Large spikes are driven

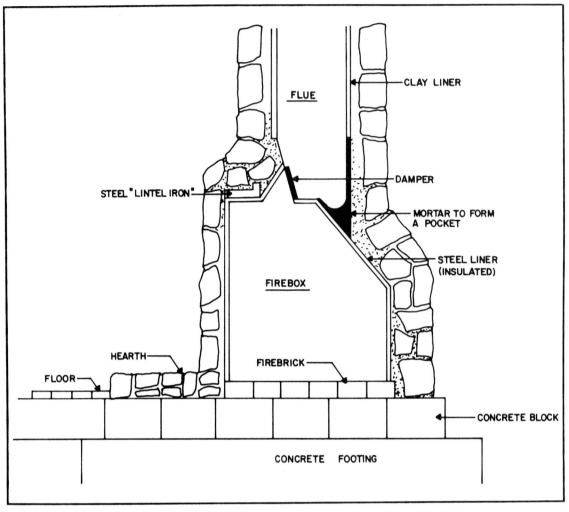

Fig. 9-6. Contemporary fireplaces often use a metal liner in place of the old masonry firebox. The liner can be regulated much more easily for various conditions and is designed to conserve more heat. It is simpler to build and the fireplace is much less likely to smoke.

into the 2 × 4's, and when the chimney is built the mortar will grip these spikes and anchor it to the wall. A hole must also be left in the wall for the stove pipe entry to the chimney. This is done by inserting a section of pipe in the wall as it is poured. The hole should be slightly larger than the stove pipe diameter so that insulation can be placed around the stovepipe. For a 6-inch pipe size use an 8-inch pipe to form the hole (Fig. 9-7).

To construct the chimney, a concrete foundation of the proper size is poured and then, after it

has hardened, mortar is mixed and a layer placed on the pad. A good mortar mix is one part cement to three parts sand. Stones are laid in the wet mortar to form the base of the chimney. Use fieldstones that have approximately 90° corners to form the corners of the chimney. About two or three layers of stone are erected and allowed to harden in place. Next, more mortar is added and stones placed, continuing to a height of about 3 feet. The clay liner is now begun. It comes in pre-cut lengths. One section is placed and the chimney built around it.

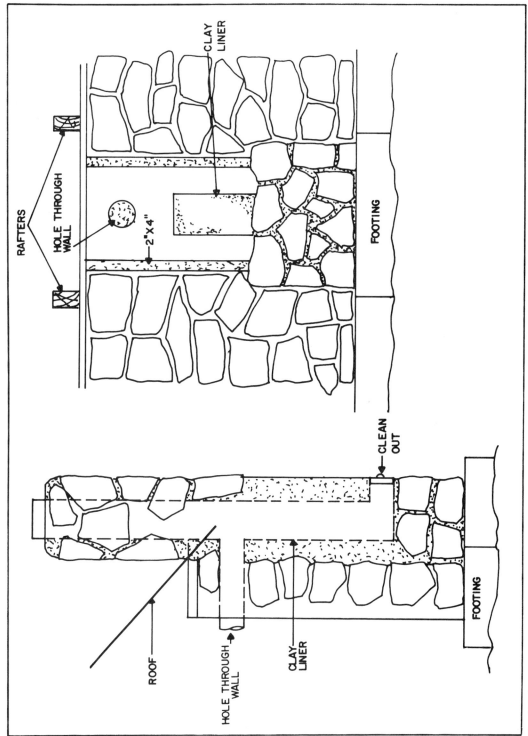

Fig. 9-7. A stone chimney may be attached to a stone wall. A hole is left in the wall for the stovepipe. The clay liner in the flue begins below this hole to function as a clean out for the chimney; 2 × 4s imbedded in the wall serve as an anchor point to attach the chimney to the house in the same manner as the porch walls were attached to the main house.

153

The liner is begun below the level of the hole in the wall and will serve later as a clean-out. Creosote and ash will collect in the bottom of the chimney and can be easily removed through a small metal clean-out door that is built into the base of the chimney.

Next, mortar is placed around the liner, which has been wrapped in a layer of fiberglass insulation, and more stones added, making sure that there is at least a 2 to 3-inch buffer of mortar between the stones and the liner. As each stage is reached, more lengths of liner are added until the chimney is topped off. Where the hole in the wall meets the chimney, a piece of clay liner is laid horizontally and attached to a hole cut in the vertical liner. (A special section of liner is used for this. The liners are cut with a masonry drill to outline the cut. Tap the section out with a hammer.)

Construction is necessarily slow if you wish to avoid the collapse of your carefully built section of stone and wet mortar. A level is used to keep the liners plumb although the outline of the outside stonework is irregular. Brick can, of course, be used to construct a chimney, and concrete block is often used, along with liners, to build a chimney.

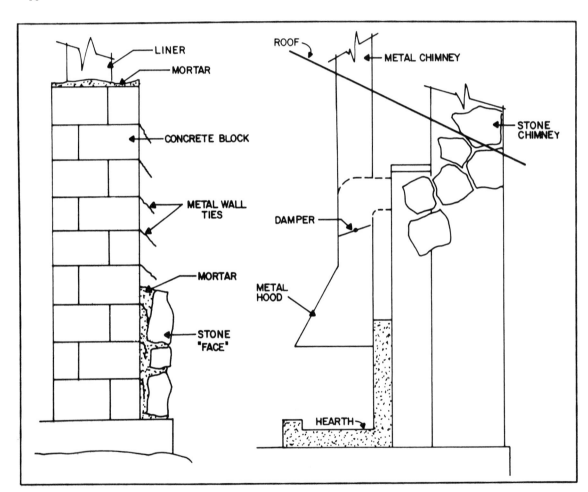

Fig. 9-8. Another method of building a stone chimney is to first construct the chimney using concrete block and then face with stone. The blocks go up quickly, are straight, and plumb. Stone and mortar is attached to the blocks using metal wall ties previously imbedded in the mortar between the blocks. A hybrid fireplace consists of a firebrick hearth with a metal hood suspended above it. The smoke exits via a metal chimney either through the roof or an exterior stone chimney.

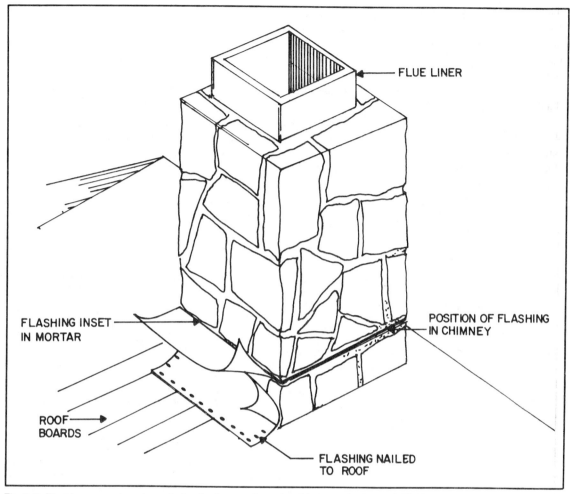

FLUE LINER

FLASHING INSET
IN MORTAR

POSITION OF FLASHING
IN CHIMNEY

ROOF
BOARDS

FLASHING NAILED
TO ROOF

Fig. 9-9. Flashing prevents water entering the house where the chimney exits the roof. Flashing was primarily made of lead sheeting but, due to increased cost, zinc flashing has become popular. Base flashing is nailed to the roof and folds up against the chimney; counter flashing is imbedded in the mortar and folds down over the base flashing.

The concrete blocks are then *faced* with a layer of stone. This method ensures a straight, solid chimney, and the stone is easily attached to the concrete blocks by the use of metal strips embedded in the mortar (Fig. 9-8).

Flashing

Where the chimney exits through the roof, *flashing* is installed to prevent the entry of water. Flashing is the term used for thin, malleable sheets of zinc or lead. At one time, lead was the traditional choice but due to cost, zinc has been replacing it. Zinc is not as

malleable as lead and isn't really suited to stone chimneys because it won't mold tightly to the contours of the chimney, which is a must for watertightness. The flashing that is fastened to the roof is called the *base flashing* and is bent upward from the roof against the chimney. *Counter flashing* is the lead flashing imbedded in the masonry of the chimney and bent downward to cover the base flashing. Underneath the flashing, roofing tar is used for a tight seal. Pointing seals the counter flashing. The roof shingles overlap the flashing on the upper side of the chimney and on either side but the base

155

flashing overlaps the shingles on the lower side of the chimney to promote runoff of water.

Counter flashing does not go all the way through the mortar. It is imbedded about 2 to 3 inches in the chimney. The joints for the counter flashing are staggerd so that there is not one solid line cut all around the chimney. Flashing is over-lapped on the corners and must be carefully instal-led to prevent a leak (Fig. 9-9).

SMOKEY FIREPLACE

Besides improper design, there are other factors that contribute to a smokey fireplace. The first is a lack of ventilation. Because modern homes are often designed with energy conservation in mind, the result is sometimes too tight a seal of insula-tion, vapor barrier, and weather stripping. Not only is there not enough air flow for the fireplace to burn well, but the inadequate air change is unhealthy for the occupants. The answer, instead of opening doors and windows in mid-winter, is to give the fireplace its own air supply that can be shut off when not needed. Simply install a vent outside, run a pipe under the floor, and emerge either in the sides of the firebox or just in front of it, in the floor. When you light a fire, open the vent. The air will flow in from the outside and be drawn into the fire, provid-ing vigorous burning.

Another cause of smoke in the house is a chim-ney built too small for the size of the firebox. As mentioned, the size of the fireplace opening and chimney are built within specific relationships. For example, the height of the opening of the firebox should be about 2/3 to 3/4 of its width. The damper should be as wide as the firebox and the depth of the firebox at least 18 inches or more. The flue should be at least 1/10 the area of the total area of the fireplace opening. Thus a fireplace measuring 3 feet wide by 2 feet high is 6 square feet in area (864 square inches). The flue area in cross section should be at minimum 1/10 of this or 86.4 square inches. To be adequate, the liner would have to be at least 8 × 12 inches (96 square inches). If your chimney is already too small you can cut down the size of the fireplace opening and achieve the same effect. A metal hood placed above the fireplace opening will often accomplish this.

Other causes include a chimney that is not high enough (at least 2-foot above a pitched roof); a damper that is too small; and local topography, such as high trees that block air flow across the chimney. Careful consideration of these factors will ensure that your fireplace will be a success when you touch a match to your first fire.

If an open fire is desired without the laborious construction of a fireplace there are other options available. There are many combination wood-stove/fireplaces on the market today that not only can be opened up like a fireplace but double as very efficient fuel burners when closed. There is the hybrid fireplace. This interesting invention uses a brick or stone hearth with a firebrick firebox and a metal hood in place of the brick throat and smoke chamber. It can be attached to a stone chim-ney or a pre-fabricated metal-type. The hearth is built into the house first and then the metal hood installed above it. The stovepipe is fed into a stone chimney or continues directly through the roof. (See Fig. 9-8).

FIREWOOD

Our house is heated entirely by wood. We have our own woodlot and it supplies all our needs for fuel. We have burned wood for 10 years and find wood heat preferable to other types such as forced air and hot water. Aside from the penetrating warmth that emanates from a woodstove, the constant mur-murings of a wood fire add life to a kitchen that a gleaming electric range just can't match.

In recent years, a great number of people have turned to wood as an alternate energy source. The rising price of oil, electrical power outages, and the increased cost of other fuels has initiated a search for dependable and cheaper alternatives. Heat con-servation techniques, solar heating, and heat from the earth are all currently being explored but by far the greatest focus has been on solid fuels, i.e., wood and coal, with wood the first choice. A boom-ing woodstove industry has arisen to meet the de-mand, and woodlot owners and operators are find-ing their trees provide an increasing amount of income.

Manufacturers of airtight woodstoves, pre-fabricated metal chimneys, and woodburning accessories such as wood splitters, creosote removers, axes, chainsaws, and so on, are all vying with each other to promote the latest "new improved" features of their products. The results are that the proud new owner of a $1000 woodstove and a $700 chimney is often unaware of the hazards involved or what is required for the day-to-day maintenance of solid fuel burners. Less-than-ethical dealers will attempt to sell low grade wood or insufficiently measured amounts to new stove owners at exorbitant prices. They very often succeed and the buyer buys half a cord of wood for the price of a full cord and discovers that aspen is not a very good firewood, despite being classed as a hardwood.

Woodlots have risen in price, are becoming increasingly hard to find, and unfortunately many are following in the footsteps of the oil and gas exploiters. Clear cutting is practiced, which completely denudes the forest of trees, giving rise to scrub growth and alienating wildlife. On an individual basis there has been a dramatic increase in the number of house fires due to inexperienced use of woodstoves and furnaces and, in some instances, shoddy materials.

What then, should a prospective wood user do to be knowledgeable in this area and also not perpetuate waste and exploitation of this resource?

First of all, if you are fortunate enough to become the owner of a woodlot, be aware that although a forest renews itself it does so slowly and can easily be reduced to a scrub area. A small woodlot of 5 to 10 acres can be decimated in as many years, whereas a larger woodlot, although bigger, can also be stripped. The forest is home for a large number of animals and birds. Fortunately, this facet of the woodland has gained considerable attention in recent years, bolstering the efforts of conservationists that have been going on for the past 100 years or longer.

As a woodlot owner, you not only have a secure base with which you can provide home heating but you have nature at your doorstep. Before buying a power saw and felling trees indiscriminately, it is good practice to become familiar with the various species of trees growing there. How long is their growth cycle, which types make the best firewood, lumber, and so on? Next, make a plan to eliminate the deadwood and thin any dense areas of trees to promote growth. By doing so, you provide your firewood, harvest efficiently, and ensure a constant supply of healthy young trees to replace those taken. This is known as *silviculture* in forestry terms, or just plain common sense.

If you are buying firewood, you should still be aware of the properties of the various species of wood available in your area, plus how to recognize a cord of wood when you see it. A *cord* of wood is a volume of wood 8 feet long, 4 feet wide, and 4 feet high. Trees are generally cut in 4-foot lengths in the woods for easy handling and stacked in piles 4-foot high by 8-foot long, giving a cord. Sometimes wood is cut 8 feet long, but this is done when most of the handling will be by machine. When buying wood, it will usually be delivered and can be ordered either in 4-foot lengths, cut into stove wood lengths (about 16 inches), or cut and split. Each is priced accordingly. If you get 4-foot lengths, you can ascertain the amount simply by piling and measuring it. If the wood is cut and split, it's more difficult to measure and you must rely on the integrity of the seller. In general, a cord will take at least two full half-ton truck loads to deliver.

If you are cutting wood yourself and using a chain saw, make the effort to learn the aspects of its safe use. Use ear and eye protectors. A chain saw is a very effective machine and I have used one extensively for 10 years. I have, however, seen a neighbor with both hands cut, another with his face split open under the eye, and a young boy dead with a severed throat. Always because of carelessness. The same concern for safety applies to using an ax. Keep it sharp. This prevents accidents due to glancing blows off a tree trunk and it cuts more efficiently. Regarding powered wood splitters, I personally find a sharp ax preferable to use. The exercise is beneficial and it is also much cheaper.

However you obtain your wood, you will need ample space to store it. Wood freshly cut is green wood and contains a large amount of water. This moisture must be removed by drying it thoroughly before burning. Dry wood gives off more heat and burns longer, and it won't create as much creosote to stick to the inside of chimneys and is the major cause of chimney fires. Wood dries best in the open air underneath a covering to protect it from rain and snow. A shed roof with open sides is an excellent way to store wood. The wood house can be a shed, separate from the house, or the house roof can be extended to form a shelter. Green wood should never be stored in an unheated basement because it will mildew and rot instead of dry. To ensure thorough drying of your firewood, it should be stacked. The larger pieces (4 inches in diameter and up) are split *before* you stack them. It takes about six months to a year for wood to air dry depending on the type of wood and the climate, so it must be obtained one year in readiness for the next.

Different species of wood have different heat-producing capacities. In general, the hardwoods are preferable to the softwoods. Most hardwoods shed their leaves, and well known ones are maple, hickory, elm, oak, beech, ash, birch, and so on. Softwoods are needle-bearing evergreens and some of these are pine, spruce, fir, hemlock, etc. Hardwoods burn longer than softwood and give off more total heat for the same amount of wood. (Dry softwood is excellent, however, for a quick hot fire when you want your pancakes in a hurry.) Hardwood is packed much more densely and it consequently weighs more than softwood when dried. It has been estimated that one cord of good air-dried hardwood is the equivalent of approximately 100 to 150 gallons of domestic fuel oil.

To acquire the information necessary to purchase and intall a woodstove, pay a visit to the nearest woodstove store. They will provide volumes of information listing the types of stoves, the features of each, how to install them, clearance factors (distances from combustible surfaces), and a host of other details concerning pre-fabricated metal chimneys, should you choose to install one of them.

Another major aspect of wood burning you should be aware of is maintenance. First the chimney. As wood burns, it releases gases that escape up the flue. Among them is a tarry substance that condenses on the inside of the chimney forming a tough, hard, shiny coating. This is creosote, and it is infamous as the cause of most chimney fires. The incidence of creosote accumulation accelerates with the use of green wood, especially softwood. Hardwood also produces creosote but in lesser amounts. Slow fires are another factor creating creosote buildup. A slow fire is the type prevalent in airtight stoves that allow only small amounts of air to feed the fire. The result is a slow burning fire that lasts all night but produces copious amounts of smoke, resulting in more creosote accumulation. The creosote builds up on the inside of the chimney and can eventually almost completely seal it off if preventative measures are not taken. The scenario that follows is this: on a windy, cold night a large fire is encouraged in the stove or fireplace to offset the chill. This fire, hotter than usual and fanned by the wind, ignites the creosote in the chimney, sometimes at the top and sometimes at the bottom. The creosote burns with a fierce intensity, shooting blue flame and sparks high above the chimney. It is a spectacular sight but only for the neighbors. The owners become agitated, to say the least, and rightly so. There is a danger of sparks igniting the house, of the chimney cracking (melting if it is a metal one), of an explosion due to a plugged flue, or, at the very least, a permanently damaged chimney. The best advice, under these conditions, is to call the fire department, close all the drafts to the stove and chimney to smother the air supply and not to throw water down the flue. Cold water down a hot flue would crack it instantly or cause it to explode, releasing the fire into the walls of your house. Keep a fire extinguisher on hand and watch for any sparks around the openings of stovepipes until the fire brigade comes to the rescue.

This can all be avoided by keeping the chimney regularly cleaned and by burning a hot fire daily. If you use an airtight, as we do, it is a good idea to begin each morning's fire by opening all the drafts and letting the fire burn hot for 15 to 20 minutes. This heats the flue and transforms any creosote from the previous night into a black, flaky ash instead of a hard tar. The ash drops down the flue and can be later removed. Every six weeks or so take down the pipes, clean them, and examine the chimney. If it needs cleaning, do so. This simple maintenance, combined with dry wood, will provide all the insurance you need against chimney fires.

Older-type fireplaces and stoves, not being airtight, are not as prone to creosote buildup since they can burn more freely. Some of the older cookstoves are beautiful to behold and if you can acquire one of them in good shape, you are indeed fortunate. We hope that your experience with wood burning will be safe and enjoyable.

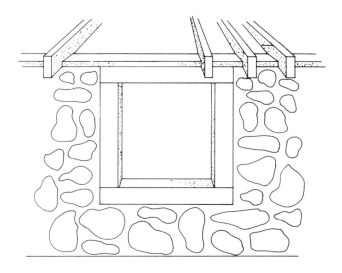

Epilogue

AFTER HAVING BUILT OUR STONE HOUSE, WE have been asked if we would do it again. Our answer is an emphatic *yes*. Yet we know of two instances where we asked owner/builders of frame houses if they would do it again and they replied no, or at least not for a long time.

This difference in outlook aroused my curiousity, and I informally surveyed some other owner/builders about their experiences with house building. Specifically I asked: "What advice would you give to a potential house builder and what have you reaped from your own efforts with regard to insights and ideas?" The majority of responses were very positive. Here are some of the insights and conclusions we received, plus some of our own.

High on the advice list is the traditional Boy Scout motto: "Be Prepared." To be prepared means engaging in the process of examining your project in great detail in order to create a vivid picture of your goal, in your mind and on paper. Then, and most importantly, allow time for your imagination to re-structure and change your concepts, thereby dis-

covering new ideas and eliminating potential errors.

Preparation means researching your project from all angles: becoming aware of any legal pitfalls, learning to pinpoint site deficiencies, and familiarizing yourself with the different aspects of construction. Thus you can search for bargains, take advantage of sales, and have the freedom to choose different options. Knowing exactly what you need makes the gathering of tools and materials much easier.

Offering design advice is difficult because design is personal expression and a part of our individuality. Some ideas can be generalized though and are straightforward. Think small, strive for quality, and ecological balance. If you have children, include them in your planning by asking them for their ideas. They see things from viewpoints we often overlook. Children appreciate having an area geared to their physical size. Such things as a child-size table and chair, low door handles, a portable step for the toilet and sink, and so on makes life easier for them and it lets them "do it myself."

Use local materials where possible and keep unnecessary frills to a minimum. Investigate the merits and disadvantages of any man-made materials and check into any potential health hazards. It is unfortunate that this last statement is necessary, but maintaining good health is up to the individual. Each of us must be aware of the negative aspects of our environment, both personal and general, and take steps to ensure that our choices are positive ones, as far as we can be certain.

Tailor your house to your lifestyle and preferences. Include features that will support ideas that are important to you. Try to have areas where each individual in the house can express themselves.

Design for the future as well as the present by allowing space that can be changed to suit expanding ideas or lifestyles: space for future children and space for a studio, when the children are grown up and gone. Your house is a reflection of your personalities and relationships and, like them, should not be static.

Regarding the personal experience of building, I asked others for their views and impressions. A good friend of ours, Roy Carnell, wrote: "Anyone can build a house if they are willing to exert the patience and extra time it takes for a beginner versus a professional. It's your attitude and confidence which has the most impact on a project—when you begin and when you hit low points in your efforts. When it all seems hopeless, refer to the facts of how much you have done, not what needs to be done. If it was easy, the banks and builders would be out of business. Put rest periods and 'pat-yourself-on-the-back' times into your game plan before you begin. Time pressures can tire you, put undue pressure on, add to mistakes, cause accidents, and take the heart out of you and your loved one.

"Avoid those who say it's not worth it or you can't do it. If you share the load with a loved one, your experience will multiply. Don't put your expectations onto your partner. Take a break if the project begins to take priority over the needs of your relationship.

"Accept the fact that the house will have faults and rough edges, and don't rely too heavily on friends or loved ones. Be happy if assistance comes, but be prepared to do it all yourself (or pay someone else)."

After reading this advice from our friend, I considered the negative responses I received from the owner/builders mentioned earlier. In both instances, there were time pressures involved. They had given themselves deadlines that were simply too short. As deadlines drew closer and their houses were not progressing as fast as they thought they should be, gnawing frustration set in and caused a bad case of the "hurries." This attitude held them in with a sense of relief instead of anticipation. Their energy was drained and in no state to embrace the demands of organizing a new home.

I have since heard of other owner/builders who have wedged themselves into this corner, or as my neighbor aptly phrases it "stuck between a big rock and a hard place." The solution is simple. Give yourself enough time, or alter your expectations to include setbacks and time extensions. Fortunately, we received such advice before we began. Building the walls was slowed due to long rainy spells, the floor joists were late from the sawmill, and the interior finish took twice as long as planned. We could have easily succumbed to despair if we hadn't been prepared.

Above all it is our attitude that ultimately decides the characteristics of our personal experience. The approach taken towards building a house accurately reflects our approach to our lives. Whether we are confident, determined, and capable of taking setbacks, or unsure, negative, and defeatist, will be evident from the start. By beginning with a confident attitude, bolstered with planning and preparation, the experience cannot help but be positive. Within each of us are latent skills and talents that will lie unused unless they are challenged. Our house has given us many things besides shelter. It has given us independence, a sense of accomplishment, and confidence in those formerly untried skills and abilities. Each year brings us new ideas and satisfactions. Our plans are ongoing and we hope that this book will serve as an impetus to action if your inclinations are in similar directions.

Index

Other Bestsellers From TAB

☐ **111 YARD AND GARDEN PROJECTS—FROM BOXES AND BINS TO TABLES AND TOOLS—Blandford**

Expert woodworker and metalcrafter Percy Blandford gives you step-by-step building guidance that's based on years of experience as a teacher and author of bestselling project guides. Plus, he provides a wealth of basic know-how on how to choose and work with wood and metal. He gives invaluable tips on constructing tool handles. And he shows how to custom design exactly the outdoor tools, accessories, and gardening aids that are right for your own particular needs!

Paper $16.95   **Hard $25.95**
Book No. 2644

☐ **CABINETS AND VANITIES—A BUILDER's HANDBOOK—Godley**

Here in easy-to-follow, step-by-step detail is everything you need to know to design, build, and install your own customized kitchen cabinets and bathroom vanities and cabinets for a fraction of the price charged by professional cabinetmakers or kitchen remodelers . . . and for less than a third of what you'd spend for the most cheaply made ready-made cabinets and vanities! 142 pp., 126 illus., 7″ × 10″.

Paper $12.95   **Hard $19.95**
Book No. 1982

☐ **58 HOME SHELVING AND STORAGE PROJECTS—Blandford**

From a two-shelf book rack or tabletop organizer to a paneled chest, basic room divider, or hall locker . . . from shelves or a spoon rack to a period reproduction of a Shaker cabinet or a Welsh dresser, you'll be amazed at the variety of projects included. And, each one includes easy-to-follow, step-by-step directions, plenty of show-how drawings, and complete materials list. 288 pp., 227 illus., 7″ × 10″.

Paper $14.95   **Book No. 1844**

☐ **HOUSE CRAFTSMANSHIP: A GUIDE TO RESTYLING AND REFURBISHING**

An information-packed sourcebook for every homeowner and do-it-yourselfer! Here are all the practical tips and step-by-step procedures you need to accomplish your restyling and refurbishing projects quickly and easily. Like having a skilled craftsman at your side. This illustrated guide shows you how to do just about every interior and exterior job imaginable, easily and inexpensively. 288 pp., 291 illus., 7″ × 10″.

Paper $14.95   **Hard $22.95**
Book No. 1809

☐ **HOW TO BE YOUR OWN ARCHITECT—2ND EDITION—Goddard and Wolverton**

The completely revised version of a long-time bestseller gives you all the expert assistance needed to design your own dream house like a professional. You'll save the money that most custom-home builders put out in architects' fees—an estimated 12% to 15% of the total construction costs—to pay for more of those "extras" you'd like your new home to include! 288 pp., 369 illus., 7″ × 10″.

Paper $14.95   **Hard $22.95**
Book No. 1790

☐ **UPHOLSTERY TECHNIQUES ILLUSTRATED—Gheen**

Here's an easy-to-follow, step-by-step guide to modern upholstery techniques that covers everything from stripping off old covers and padding to restoring and installing new foundations, stuffing, cushions, and covers. All the most up-to-date pro techniques are included along with lots of time- and money-saving "tricks-of-the-trade" not usually shared by professional upholsterers. 352 pp., 549 illus., 7″ × 10″.

Paper $16.95   **Hard $27.95**
Book No. 2602

☐ **DO-IT-YOURSELF DESIGNER WINDOWS**

If the cost of custom-made draperies puts you in a state of shock . . . if you've had trouble finding window coverings of any kind for cathedral or other problem windows . . . or if you're unsure of what type of window decor would look right in your home . . . here's all the advice and information you've been searching for. It's a complete, hands-on guide to selecting, measuring, making, and installing just about any type of window treatment imaginable. You'll even get an expert's insight into selection and installation of decorative storm windows and thermal windows, stained glass windows, woven or wooden blinds, and workable treatments for problem areas. 272 pp., 414 illus., 7″ × 10″.

Paper $14.95   **Hard $21.95**
Book No. 1922

☐ **PRACTICAL LANDSCAPING AND LAWN CARE—Webb**

Make your lawn the envy of the entire neighborhood . . . *without* spending a fortune or putting in never-ending hours of maintenance time! Here's absolutely everything you need to successfully plan, plant, and maintain lawn grasses and groundcovers, vines, and flowering ornamentals . . . annual, biennial, and perennial flowers . . . shade trees, lawn trees . . . even decorative (and delicious!) fruits and berries. It doesn't matter whether your climate is cold and damp or hot and dry . . . whether your soil is sandy, rocky, or gummy clay . . . *everything* you need is here! 240 pp., 84 illus., 7″ × 10″.

Paper $13.95   **Hard $21.95**
Book No. 1818

☐ **HOW TO BUILD YOUR OWN UNDERGROUND HOME—2ND EDITION—Scott**

What is an underground home? What types of construction options are available for underground building? What are the advantages of building an underground home in the first place? Well, here's where to find the answers: Step-by-step, over-the-shoulder instructions and advice that even a first-time homebuilder can follow; Fully illustrated and detailed construction drawings and photos of projects built by the author; Loads of important money-saving tips; Dozens of lighting, carpeting, and interior garden ideas! 224 pp., 196 illus., 7″ × 10″.

Paper $11.95   **Hard $19.95**
Book No. 1792

Other Bestsellers From TAB

☐ **PROFESSIONAL PLUMBING TECHNIQUES— ILLUSTRATED AND SIMPLIFIED—Smith**

This plumber's companion includes literally everything about plumbing you'll ever need! From changing a washer to installing new fixtures; it covers installing water heaters, water softeners, dishwashers, gas stoves, gas dryers, grease traps, clean outs, and more. Includes piping diagrams, tables, charts, and arranged alphabetically. 294 pp., 222 illus.

Hard $16.95   **Book No. 1763**

☐ **SUPERINSULATED, TRUSS-FRAME HOUSE CON-STRUCTION**

A revolutionary home building technique that's faster and easier to construct . . . and far less expensive than traditional methods! If you're planning to build or buy a new home . . . or wish you could . . . this book will show you how superinsulated, truss-frame construction can mean having the high-quality, energy-efficient home you want at a fraction of the price you'd expect! 240 pp., 244 illus., 7″ × 10″.

Paper $15.50   **Hard $21.95**
Book No. 1674

☐ **MASTERING HOUSEHOLD ELECTRICAL WIRING— Kittle**

Now you can add ultra-modern conveniences to your home, such as a handy electric garage door opener, extra outdoor outlets, a brand *new* door-chime, and more—without paying the high cost of an electrical contractor. Step-by-step instructions, photos and diagrams of work-in progress show you how to handle large and small electrical jobs with no prior experience. 304 pp., 326 illus., 7″ × 10″.

Paper $13.95   **Book No. 1587**

☐ **BUILDING A LOG HOME FROM SCRATCH OR KIT—Ramsey**

A step-by-step guide to planning, designing, and constructing a modern, energy-efficient log dwelling! Find out how you can *save even more by building your own log house* either from scratch or from a kit! All the how-to's you need are included in this exciting new guide that takes you from the initial planning stages right through the final interior finishing. 256 pp., 257 illus.

Paper $12.95   **Book No. 1458**

☐ **WHAT'S IT WORTH? A HOME INSPECTION AND APPRAISAL MANUAL—Scaduto**

Here's a guide that can save home buyers and home owners thousands of dollars in unexpected maintenance and repair costs! You'll find out what types of structural problems occur in older and in new homes, even condominiums . . . covers everything from foundations and crawl spaces to attics and roofs . . . learn simple "tricks of the trade" for spotting problems and discover how professional appraisal techniques can be applied to any home! 256 pp., 281 illus., 7″ × 10″.

Paper $12.95   **Hard $21.95**
Book No. 1761

☐ **CONSTRUCTING AND MAINTAINING YOUR WELL AND SEPTIC SYSTEM—Alth**

A practical, money-saving guide for do-it-yourself homebuilders, homesteaders, and non-urban homeowners! Here, in step-by-step format, is all the information you need to plan and construct and maintain efficient water and septic units that will stand up to your needs for many years to come. Even if you're not interested in doing all or part of the work yourself, this guide can still prove an important money-saver by showing you what should be done and how it should be done, so you can deal more effectively with professional well drillers and septic contractors. 240 pp., 206 illus., 7″ × 10″.

Paper $12.95   **Hard $19.95**
Book No. 1654

☐ **BE YOUR OWN CONTRACTOR: THE AFFORDABLE WAY TO HOME OWNERSHIP—Alth**

If you've put your dreams of home ownership on "hold" because of today's sky-high building costs, this single guidebook can change all that! It shows you can save thousands of dollars on the cost of a new home by becoming your own contractor. It shows *how* to build an attractive, secure, comfortable home at minimum cost. 256 pp., 207 illus., 7″ × 10″.

Paper $12.95   **Book No. 1554**

*Prices subject to change without notice.

Look for these and other TAB books at your local bookstore.

TAB BOOKS Inc.
P.O. Box 40
Blue Ridge Summit, PA 17214

Send for FREE TAB catalog describing over 1200 current titles in print.